WILDFLOWERS of the CANADIAN ROCKIES

A Field Guide
to Wildflowers of
Banff National Park
Bow Valley Provincial Park
Hamber Provincial Park
Jasper National Park
Kananaskis Country
Kootenay National Park
Mt. Assiniboine Provincial Park
Mt. Robson Provincial Park
Waterton Lakes National Park
Yoho National Park
and Surrounding Areas

George W. Scotter & Hälle Flygare

WILDFLOWERS of the CANADIAN ROCKIES

Hurtig Publishers
Edmonton

Hurtig Publishers Ltd.
10560–105 Street
Edmonton, Alberta
Canada T5H 2W7

Canadian Cataloguing in Publication Data

Scotter, G.W. (George Wilby)
Wildflowers of the Canadian Rockies

Includes index.
ISBN 0-88830-285-1 (bound).—ISBN
0-88830-286-X (pbk.)

1. Wild flowers—Rocky Mountains, Canadian–
Identification.* I. Flygare, Hälle, 1936–
II. Title.
QK203.R63S36 1986 582.13′09711 C85-091513-9

Editor: José Druker
Design: David Shaw & Associates Ltd.
Composition: Attic Typesetting Inc.
Printed and bound in Canada
by Friesen Printers

Dedicated to Etta and Linda,
who share our love and enjoyment
of nature

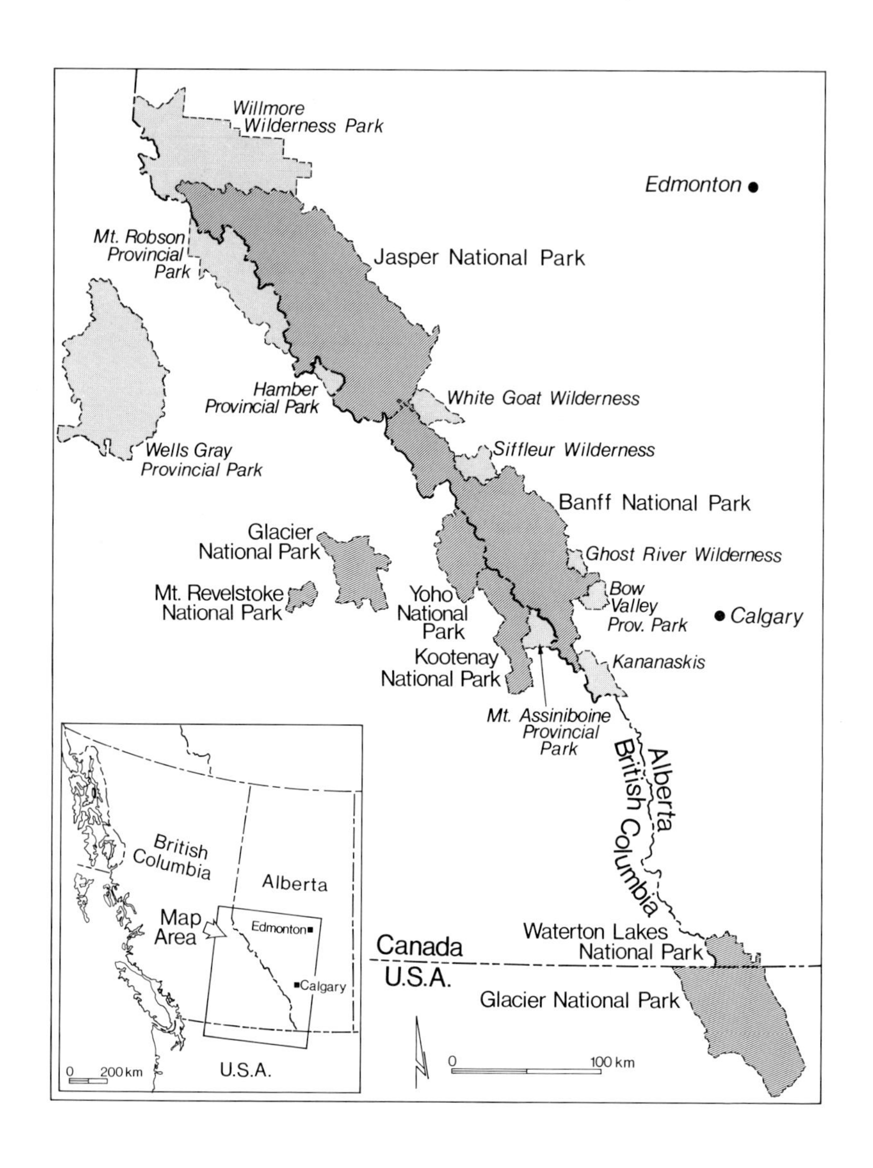

Figure 1. The Southern Canadian Rocky Mountains

Contents

Acknowledgements

We owe a debt of gratitude to a number of colleagues and friends who contributed to this field guide. Bill Cody, Derek Johnson, and Job Kuijt verified identifications of some plants illustrated in the photographs. The manuscript was read and many useful suggestions were made by Bill Cody, Diane Griffin, Julie Hrapko, and Kevin Van Tighem. Simon Lunn kindly loaned a photograph of Western Wake Robin for inclusion in this book. Much insight was gained on local plant distributions in Waterton Lakes National Park from Ken Goble. Special appreciation goes to Shirley MacDougall and Susan Popowich, who volunteered their personal time in typing the manuscript and preparing the illustrations, respectively.

Introduction

Much of the colour and beauty of the Canadian Rocky Mountains is derived from the wildflowers that thrive there. People are amazed by the flourishing variety of brilliantly coloured flowers that attract their attention during the summer months. Most people have a desire to know more about them, feeling that this will enrich their aesthetic appreciation of their environment.

This conveniently sized field guide has been written to enable the general public in the many national parks, provincial parks, and wilderness areas within the southern Canadian Rocky Mountains to recognize some of the hundreds of wildflowers they may encounter, whether along the highways and hiking trails or near campgrounds and in the towns.

Having worked in the Canadian Rocky Mountains for many years, we have some idea as to what the millions of visitors and residents in the region are looking for in a wildflower book. Our goal has been to keep this field guide simple and enjoyable reading but accurate in detail. Therefore, only a minimal amount of the technical jargon of a plant taxonomist has been employed to enable the non-specialists to enter easily into the botanist's world.

This field guide contains over 260 coloured photographs and describes 228 species, representing 41 families, all of them found in the southern Canadian Rockies, which we often refer to as "our area." As there are more than 1500 plants in the southern Canadian Rocky Mountains, there are many that are not mentioned. Our aim was to make this field guide comprehensive enough to suit a wide range of users without making it too cumbersome. Many of the plants we have included are the most showy, familiar, and common that people will encounter. We felt prompted, however, to share with our readers a few of our discoveries of rare plants within the Canadian Rockies. We hope that as users become familiar with the more common wildflowers, they will be stimulated to search for and enjoy the beauty and wonders of some of our rarer plants.

In keeping with the spirit of this book, there are no botanical keys. For simplicity we have arranged the plants by flower colour. Each plant is listed by its familiar name and some other common names by which it might be known, as well as by its family, genus, and species name. Identification is based entirely on comparison of the unknown plant with a photograph and brief description.

Use this field guide in the following ways: Look carefully at a flower to determine its colour and general characteristics. Turn to the relevant colour section and scan the photographs for a flower that looks similar. Compare the real flower with the picture and then with the description. If your plant does not fit the description, then try again. In seeking to identify the plant, look for characteristics such as plant size, leaf arrangement and shape, numbers and arrangement of sepals, petals and other flower parts, as well as other features described in this guide. If you vaguely recognize the plant, you might try going first to the index of common names or scientific names, which will refer you to the relevant page for comparison of your plant with the picture and description.

The wildflowers are arranged in four colour groups as follows: (1) green to white, including cream; (2) yellow; (3) pink to red and orange; and (4) purple to blue, including lavender. Arbitrary decisions had to be made between groups because some flowers are intermediate in colour or show a range of variation at different stages of maturation or even on the same inflorescence. No one section is so large that determination is difficult, though it is advisable to check more than one section if colour deviation is suspected.

Identification by colour photograph has its limitations, but in most cases each photograph will lead the reader directly to the exact species, or in those instances where a large number of species is involved, to the genus.

A multiplicity of common names may occur for many species, often varying from province to province and country to country. There has never been a list of common names that has succeeded in gaining acceptance over any wide area. Instead, many plants have acquired local names in the different areas in which they grow. Thus *Calypso bulbosa* goes by nine names including "Calypso Orchid," "Venus Slipper," and "Fairy Slipper" in different parts of Alberta and British Columbia, whereas elsewhere it has still other names. In this book, the common names employed are those that have enjoyed fairly wide acceptance in our area and follow the names applied by recent identification manuals (see selected references).

Botanists use scientific names for plants because they are far more consistent and precise than common names and because they are understood by others all over the world. Each botanical name consists of two parts, comparable to the way in which we give names to people belonging to different families. In plant names, however, the first part tells the genus (group) to which the plant belongs; for example, *Rosa*, which means a rose. This is the same as a surname or family name, such as Jones. The second part of the botanical name indicates the species (particular member of the group); for example, *acicularis*, which means "with needle-like prickles." This is comparable to the given name of an individual, such as Tom in Tom Jones. The Latin names used here generally follow *Flora of Alberta*, by Moss, or *A Flora of Waterton Lakes National Park*, by Kuijt.

While our goal has been to keep technical terminology to an absolute minimum, there is a need for readers to understand the basic structure of a plant and the parts that form a flower. A glossary and a few flower diagrams have been included to assist the reader in understanding flower structure and types.

For all of the species described and illustrated we have added observations about their distribution within the Canadian Rocky Mountains. The distribution of wildflowers is generally well known in our national parks but far less known in provincial parks and wilderness areas. For that reason we have given distributions for Banff (B), Jasper (J), Kootenay (K), Waterton Lakes (W), and Yoho (Y) national parks. Distributions in provincial parks and wilderness areas can be judged by their proximity to these national parks.

As flowering times vary so much according to altitude, latitude, and other ecological conditions, and because the growing season is so short in the Rocky Mountains, no attempt has been made to include this information for all species. The Rocky Mountain region is a vertical land where spring and summer ascend the slopes and a flower that blooms in May in the river valleys might not flower until July or even later at higher altitudes. For example, the Glacier Lily blooms in Waterton Lakes National Park during early May, but can be found flowering at Highwood Pass in Kananaskis Country during August.

We have not discriminated between native plants and introduced plants, many of the latter being among today's common species. On the other hand, we have not included in this book the trees, ferns, horsetails, grasses, sedges, or rushes.

To add interest to the field guide, we have added supplemental notes on use of the plants by wildlife as well as past and present use by humans, which we have determined from personal observations or from a study of the literature. A vast lore of practical plant applications was passed down among the indigenous people generation to generation, some of the knowledge eventually coming to the early white settlers. Some historical and pioneering uses of various plants are discussed in the text as a matter of interest. Those wishing to ferret out more information on a specific subject should consult the excellent works mentioned in the selected references.

It is not our intent to encourage use of wild plants unless they are abundant and outside a protected area. Know which ones are abundant and take care in their use. Never eat plants you are not absolutely sure are safe and do not allow children to handle plants which might possibly prove to be poisonous.

Remember that wildflowers within our parks and wilderness areas are protected by law and should not be picked or removed. However, this does not prevent the enthusiast from looking at them, photographing them, enjoying them as they are, and leaving them to give similar pleasure to those who follow. There is a challenge in looking for different kinds of wildflowers in their native habitat without depriving the next passerby of similar enjoyment. Our wildflowers are for all to enjoy today and for future generations to enjoy tomorrow.

We believe that the coloured photographs, non-technical descriptions, and convenient size will make this field guide useful to the backpacker, mountain climber, highway traveller, and generally curious-minded. We have succeeded if we have introduced you to some of the treasures and gems waiting to be discovered in our Rocky Mountain inheritance. Being able to recognize the plants you encounter and to call them by name is an indispensable and exciting first step in a deeper understanding and appreciation of the natural world around us.

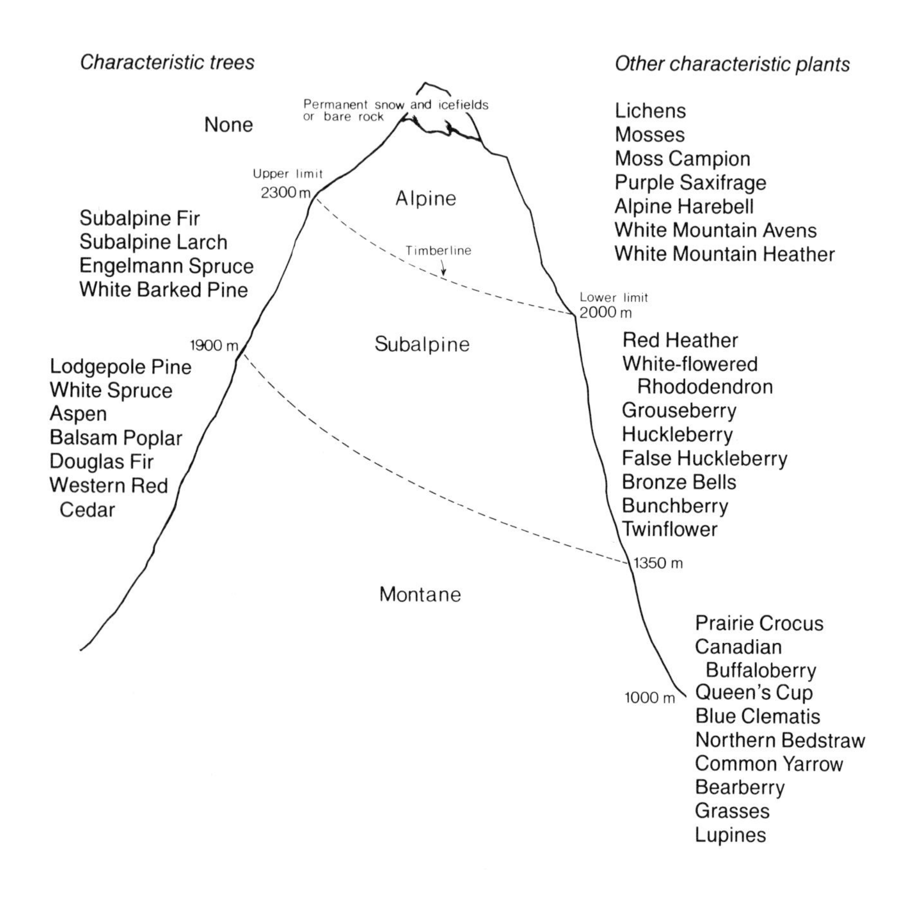

Figure 2. Vegetation zones of the southern Canadian Rocky Mountains with examples of characteristic plants and trees

Vegetation Zones

At first glance the trees and forests of the southern Canadian Rocky Mountains look like a continuous green carpet rolling up the mountainsides. Upon closer inspection three major vegetation zones, each with its own characteristic plants and animals, reveal themselves.

These zones form bands across the mountainsides—somewhat like the layers of a wedding cake. The bottom band, called the montane, is found in the valley bottoms. The subalpine forms the middle layer. The upper band, the alpine, is the land above the trees. One zone merges into another and there is much overlapping because of different topography, exposure, moisture, soil, and prevailing winds.

The wildflower enthusiast who learns to recognize these zones will soon discover that certain plants can be expected to be found in a specific zone. This knowledge that certain plants belong to certain altitudes and in certain zones will help in the discovery of new flowers as well as in identifying unfamiliar ones.

The more or less distinct altitudinal zonation is due, in part, to the gradual lowering of temperature from the lowland to the summit of a mountain. The lower part of most mountains is densely wooded, whereas the upper part may be treeless. At higher elevations, the trees become more stunted, and the upper limit of trees, or timberline, is generally quite distinct. On the warmer south side of a mountain, timberline is often several hundred metres higher than on the cooler and more shaded north side.

Precipitation also greatly affects the plant cover of mountains. Thus, the eastern foothills situated in the rain shadow of the Rocky Mountains may be treeless and inhabited by drought-resistant prairie species, while the western foothills in British Columbia are covered with trees. Precipitation usually increases with altitude. This explains why some of the richest and most lush assemblages of Rocky Mountain wildflowers may be found above timberline, in sheltered alpine valleys where the plant cover is well protected by a deep blanket of snow in winter but in summer is abundantly supplied with water from melting snowbanks. Another characteristic of the eastern slopes is the warm chinook wind that can deplete the snow cover several times during a winter.

The major zones in the southern Canadian Rocky Mountains are shown in Figure 2 and a brief description follows.

Wetlands of the montane zone

Shrublands and White Spruce communities in the montane zone

Grasslands and Aspen communities in the montane zone

Montane Zone

The montane zone occurs from the lowest elevations in the southern Canadian Rockies at about 1000 m above sea level. Its upper elevations vary, depending on location and aspect. For example, the upper boundary is 1900 m on warm, southerly and westerly aspects in Kootenay National Park, and about 1350 m in Jasper National Park.

The forests of the montane zone, the beginning of the mountain forests, are generally dominated by Douglas Fir and White Spruce, which often follow the fire-induced Lodgepole Pine and Aspen forests. However, on some dry sites, Lodgepole Pine forms forests which are not replaced by other trees. Western Red Cedar, Western Larch, and the occasional Ponderosa Pine are present in southeastern British Columbia.

On the driest montane sites, grasslands form the mature vegetation. Fire appears to be important in maintaining these grasslands. The Fescue grasslands occur in the foothills and valley bottoms on the eastern side of the Rocky Mountains. Rough Fescue dominates the grasslands with secondary quantities of Parry Oat Grass. Farther north, the grasslands are dominated by Northern Wheatgrass, June Grass, and Plains Reed Grass. Wheatgrass communities are present in southeastern British Columbia.

Numerous shrubs are found at this zone, especially Canadian Buffaloberry, Common Juniper, Creeping Juniper, Snowberry, Silverberry, Prickly Rose, Wild Gooseberry, Bracted Honeysuckle, Saskatoon, Red Osier Dogwood, Shrubby Cinquefoil, Chokecherry, Bearberry, and various willows. Shrubs become more important as moisture increases. They usually occur in suitable niches on north-facing slopes, in ravines, and in groundwater seepage areas.

Many wildflowers typical of the foothills and prairies are present in the montane zone. Some of these are the Nodding Onion, Wild Gaillardia, Wild Flax, Blue Clematis, Red and White Baneberry, Northern Bedstraw, Three-flowered Avens, Shooting Star, Western Meadow Rue, Star-flowered Solomon's Seal, Common Fireweed, Pearly Everlasting, Blue Beardtongue, asters, fleabanes, goldenrods, hedysarums, paintbrushes, vetches, and many others.

Extensive wetland complexes have developed along floodplains and are characterized by a mosaic of mixed forests, willow fens, and sedge meadows.

Subalpine Zone

The subalpine zone receives more rain and snow than the montane zone and hence supports a heavier growth of coniferous trees. It occurs at altitudes above the montane zone and below the unforested alpine zone. The subalpine zone can be further divided into lower and upper subalpine. The predominant vegetation of the lower subalpine is a dense, closed coniferous forest. Mature forest is dominated by Engelmann Spruce and Subalpine Fir. Lodgepole Pine forests are also common at lower altitudes.

The upper subalpine portion, characterized by open forests and meadows, is intermediate between lower subalpine closed forest and treeless alpine tundra. Compared to the lower subalpine, the upper subalpine climate is cooler and wetter, with greater snowfall, later snowmelt, and a shorter growing season. High winds also appear to be a significant climatic factor, pruning the trees into characteristic stunted forms called "elfin wood" or krummholz. The only tree to escape this stunting is the deciduous Subalpine Larch, occurring from Lake Louise south within our area; its needles turn to a brilliant golden yellow in the autumn.

In the lower subalpine the trees grow so tall and so close together that little light reaches the forest floor. Consequently the ground vegetation consists of a thick carpet of feather mosses and lichens. There is a scattering of shade-tolerant shrubs like White-flowered Rhododendron, Grouseberry, Huckleberry, False Huckleberry, and Green Alder. Shrubs of the Heather Family, such as White Mountain Heather, Red Heather, and Yellow Heather, are common in the more open forests near treeline. Some of the characteristic herbaceous plants include Bronze Bells, Bunchberry, One-flowered Clintonia, Twinflower, and several wintergreens.

Wildflowers in the subalpine zone

Engelmann Spruce in the subalpine zone

Subalpine Larch near timberline in the subalpine zone

Krummholz or "elfin wood" at timberline

Carex meadow in the low alpine zone (Photo courtesy of George Scotter)

Heather community above timberline in the low alpine zone

Wildflowers and shrubs in the alpine zone

Alpine Zone

Between the coniferous forest and the barren rocky peaks of the mountains is a zone in which herbaceous plants exist but in which no trees of any significance can grow. This is the alpine zone. It is colder, more exposed to wind, and receives heavier precipitation than the other zones. Tree growth is prevented by a combination of long, cold winters, short, cool summers, and high winds. Vegetation is characterized by a mosaic of low shrub and herb communities in the lower alpine zone and by lichens and xerophytic mosses, which are able to withstand extreme temperature ranges and desiccation, in the upper alpine zone. There is little or no vascular vegetation growing at the highest elevations.

Dwarf shrub tundra dominated by Yellow Heather, White Mountain Heather, Arctic Willow, and White Mountain Avens is characteristic of lower alpine altitudes. Dense mats of sedge prevail in depressions where the snow is deep and melts late.

Many of the plants take on special growth forms to make the most of what heat and moisture falls upon them. They include prostrate forms growing along the surface of the ground; cushion plants that wedge themselves in crevices; and leathery or hairy-leaved forms, which are adapted to conserve water by reducing the desiccation of growing shoots caused by wind. The shortness of the growing season and the severity of winter favour fast-growing perennials. Such hardy plants form the truly alpine and arctic element of the flora.

A few of the more conspicuous species in the alpine zone are Purple Saxifrage, Moss Campion, Alpine Rockcress, Mountain Sorrel, Alpine Lousewort, Contorted Lousewort, and the shrubs already mentioned. Some subalpine wildflowers work their way up into the low alpine zone, as do several shrubs.

Green, White & Cream Flowers

Western Anemone; Chalice Flower; Towhead Babies BJKWY*

Anemone occidentalis BUTTERCUP FAMILY

These large, cream-white flowers, with a bluish cast underneath, open early in the spring, as their leaves are beginning to emerge. Borne on woolly stems, the flowers brighten the slopes with their showy cups, half-filled with stamens that wreath their centres like golden crowns. Grey-green feathery leaves below the bloom expand during the summer. The sepals soon fall and are followed by a tousled top of plumed seeds at the tip of now tall stems. The plants are sometimes called "towhead babies" because of the fuzzy appearance of the fruiting heads. The fall winds carry away the seeds, whose feathery tails act as parachutes in the dispersal to new habitats. Western Anemone is a characteristic plant of wet alpine meadows and clearings of the timberline zone where snow remains late.

White Globe Flower BJKW

Trollius albiflorus [*T. laxus*] BUTTERCUP FAMILY

This handsome plant has individual, snowy white flowers, about 4 cm across, with golden centres. Lacking petals, these flowers consist of 5 to 10 petal-like sepals, bright yellow stamens, and green pistils. The undersides of the sepals have a rose-green tinge, which is most easily seen when the flowers are partly closed. At this stage they look like small globes, as suggested by the common name. The glistening, rich green leaves, deeply 5- to 7-parted, are mostly at the base of the stem. The top-shaped pod contains several seeds. White Globe Flower is common in wet alpine meadows and along marshy borders of alpine and subalpine streams.

Drummond's Anemone BJKWY

Anemone drummondii [*A. lithophila*] BUTTERCUP FAMILY

Another elegant member of the alpine community, this plant flowers near the edge of retreating snowbanks. A cluster of petioled, deeply dissected basal leaves grows from a thick, branched rootstock. Midway up the stem there is a collar of similar but smaller leaves. All above-ground parts of the plant are protected by fine woolly hairs. The striking flowers are creamy white inside and tinged with pastel blue on the outside. Each solitary flower, which is short-lived, consists of 5 to 7 sepals and numerous pistils and stamens; there are no petals. The transitory flowers are soon replaced by tiny woolly "thimbles" containing round, black achenes.

*Indicates distribution. See Introduction for explanation of letters.

Western Anemone

Western Anemone

White Globe Flower

Drummond's Anemone

Fringed Grass-of-Parnassus

BJKWY

Parnassia fimbriata

GRASS-OF-PARNASSUS FAMILY

The snowy white, buttercup-like blooms of Fringed Grass-of-Parnassus are borne singly on stems 15 to 35 cm tall, with a clasping leaf-like bract about halfway up the stem. The showy flower has 5 petals, each with 5 to 7 conspicuous green veins and fringed lower edges. A rosette of glossy green, kidney- or heart-shaped leaves spreads from a perennial rootstock. Five white, fertile stamens alternate with 5 gland-tipped, sterile ones, which are yellow in colour. The plant's fruit is a many-seeded, 4-valved capsule. Favourite haunts of the plant are wet mossy areas along creeks, springs, and lakeshores in valleys to above timberline, where it is often found in dense colonies.

Star-flowered Solomon's Seal

BJKWY

Smilacina stellata

LILY FAMILY

Each unbranched stem of this elegant little plant supports 7 to 13 stiffly arranged, pale blue-green leaves. The leaves are strongly veined and they zigzag up the stem. A few to several widely spaced flowers are borne at the tip. These are star-shaped flowers of the purest white. They have 6 petals, which are longer than the stamens. The fruits of this plant take the form of berries. At first the berries are greenish, marked with 3 red stripes, but they turn nearly black when ripe. The powdered root was reportedly applied to wounds to help in the clotting of blood. Star-flowered Solomon's Seal is widespread and can be seen in woodlands and open meadows.

Rough-fruited Fairybell

BJKWY

Disporum trachycarpum

LILY FAMILY

This common woodland plant has crinkly-edged, veiny leaves, almost as wide as they are long, which clasp around the stalks. From 1 to 4 whitish to greenish-yellow flowers droop from the tips of the slender stalks. The flowers are like little bells in bud, but they are much more ragged when fully open. They give way to bright orange-red berries with wart-like projections on the surface. Although other lily species produce poisonous fruit, these berries are edible either cooked or raw. Fairybells bloom in spring and early summer.

Fringed Grass-of-Parnassus

Fringed Grass-of-Parnassus

Star-flowered Solomon's Seal

Rough-fruited Fairybell

White Mountain Heather — BJKY

Cassiope mertensiana — HEATH FAMILY

Often associated with Red Heather and Yellow Heather, this dwarf evergreen shrub occurs in mats that carpet the ground near timberline and below moist snowbed slopes well into the alpine region. The ends of the branches bear a profusion of nodding, bell-shaped, snow-white flowers, sometimes tinged with rose. Red-tipped sepals add a touch of colour to each bell. The petals of the perfect little bells are slightly rolled back from the rim, which helps distinguish this plant from Yellow Heather, whose petals are constricted near the rim. Minute scale-like leaves are arranged in 4 distinct rows and overlap one another like fish scales or cedar leaves. The stalks are curved when they bear the flowers, but become erect as the seed capsules mature. Because of its high resin content, this plant can be used as fuel for fires. Its branches are reported to produce a golden-brown dye. Rocky Mountain White Heather (*C. tetragona*) looks very similar except for a deep groove that runs the length of the lower leaf surface.

Woolly Pussytoes; Woolly Everlasting — BJKWY

Antennaria lanata — COMPOSITE FAMILY

Several species of this genus grow in the Rocky Mountains of southern Canada. They are difficult to distinguish from one another. As suggested by the common name, Woolly Pussytoes has leaves and stems that are closely appressed with whitish, woolly hairs that give the plant a pale grey to greyish-green colour. The rosettes of basal leaves arise from fibrous, creeping stems; the stem leaves, often with brown, nail-like tips, are quite small in size. This plant's 4 to 10 tiny flowers are arranged in heads at the tip of the stem. Each head forms a compact, rounded cluster and is surrounded by bracts, which are dark-coloured below with pale tips. The long-lasting quality of the flowers makes them popular for dried arrangements. Woolly Pussytoes grows in moist alpine and subalpine meadows.

Tall White Bog Orchid; Fragrant White Orchid — BJKWY

Habenaria dilatata — ORCHID FAMILY

This graceful orchid is one that you cannot fail to stop and admire. The flowers are gleaming white, 2 to 3 cm wide, and 20 or more of them will be clustered 70 to 100 cm above the ground, near the top of a smooth stem. The lip of the flower, conspicuously widened at the base, narrows toward the tip. A spur, usually as long as the lip, projects backward from the rest of the flower. The waxy whiteness of the flower is enhanced by 2 yellow stamens. Tall White Bog Orchid is strongly perfumed, like a blending of cloves, vanilla, and mock orange. The rather succulent leaves, up to 20 cm long, decrease in size the further up the stem they are. Bogs, wet ditches, and seepages are favoured habitats for this regal beauty.

White Mountain Heather

Woolly Pussytoes

Tall White Bog Orchid

Hooded Lady's Tresses BJKWY

Spiranthes romanzoffiana ORCHID FAMILY

Hooded Lady's Tresses is one of the most common orchids in the Rocky Mountains. A characteristic feature is the crowded flower spike, which is so tightly twisted as to produce 3-ranked rows of overlapping, creamy white flowers. Like other orchids, each flower consists of 3 sepals and 3 petals, with the stamens and pistil combined into one unit. The upper sepals and petals are united into an overhanging hood that looks like the peak of an old-fashioned sunbonnet. Some flower lovers feel that the spiral spike bears a fanciful resemblance to neatly braided hair; hence the common name. Check this quaint orchid's flowers for a strong vanilla-like scent. The broad grass-like leaves, 5 to 15 cm long, are mostly near the base of the stem. This plant is found in wet meadows, seepage areas, and on damp grassy slopes.

False Mitrewort; Foam Flower BJKW

Tiarella unifoliata SAXIFRAGE FAMILY

Large maple-like leaves characterize this perennial herb, which is 10 to 40 cm tall and has a loose spray of delicate white or creamy white flowers. The long-petioled basal leaves, between 3 and 9 cm across, arise from a rootstock. They have 3 to 5 lobes with prominent double-toothed margins. The flowering stem, with gland-tipped, white hairs on the upper portion, bears a similar but smaller leaf. A dozen or so flowers, usually in groups of 3, are arranged on the delicate stalks well above the leaves. False Mitrewort's small lacy flower consists of 5 pinkish-white sepals, 5 white to creamy petals, 1 pistil with 2 long styles, and 10 protruding stamens. The white filaments of the stamens are a conspicuous feature; 5 are longer than the calyx lobes and 5 are shorter. The seed pod has a rather odd shape and has been compared to a tiara worn by royalty, thus giving rise to the generic name *Tiarella*, meaning little tiara. Search for large clumps of this dainty beauty in sheltered places in woods, especially along streams.

Contorted Lousewort; Coiled Lousewort BKWY

Pedicularis contorta FIGWORT FAMILY

The lousewort group is known for the unusual shape of its flowers, and the 2-parted flower of Contorted Lousewort is the most spectacular of them all. Bright creamy-white flowers are scattered along a stem 8 to 12 cm long. The long, downward-coiled, upper lip of the corolla tube is curved like a shepherd's crook and twisted sideways near its tip. The upper lip is partially enclosed by the 2 lobes of the lower lip. The fern-like basal leaves are toothed, and stem leaves alternate along the stem, decreasing in size towards the top of the plant. These feathery leaves are green and often wine-tinged. Small clumps of this showy plant are found in alpine meadows and on open slopes below timberline.

Hooded Lady's Tresses

False Mitrewort

Contorted Lousewort

Red Osier Dogwood

BJKWY

Cornus stolonifera

DOGWOOD FAMILY

This willow-like shrub, between 1 and 3 m tall, often forms nearly impenetrable thickets along streams and rivers and in moist forests. The reddish bark, which becomes a much brighter red when subjected to winter frost, is distinctive. The heavily veined leaves, dark green above and paler beneath, are egg-shaped with rounded bases and pointed ends. These leaves handsomely set off the flat-topped cluster of small, greenish-white flowers. Each flower has 4 small sepals, 4 spreading, oval-shaped petals, 4 stamens, and a club-shaped pistil. By early autumn the clusters of globular white fruit, often tinged with blue, contrast with the brilliant plum-coloured leaves and deep-red branches. The branches were used by Indians for weaving baskets, and the inner bark served in a tobacco mixture and for making tea.

Alpine Spring Beauty

BW

Claytonia megarhiza

PURSLANE FAMILY

As the scientific name *megarhiza* suggests, this plant grows from a fleshy, swollen taproot rather than from a corm. Alpine Spring Beauty in bloom is very similar to Western Spring Beauty, but may be distinguished by its tufts of spoon-shaped, reddish-green, basal leaves. The exquisite pink to white flowers are often obscured by narrow stem leaves. Both the leaves and stems are usually tinged with red. This glamorous and rather rare plant, confined to alpine scree slopes, flowers in mid-summer.

Red Osier Dogwood

Red Osier Dogwood

Alpine Spring Beauty

Chokecherry

BJKWY

Prunus virginiana

ROSE FAMILY

Chokecherry is a conspicuous white-flowering shrub or small tree, up to 10 m tall, which is common in thickets, in open woods, and along streams. Attached by stout petioles, the leaves are 5 to 10 cm long, egg-shaped to broadly oval, with sharp, marginal teeth. The 5-petaled flowers, about 1 cm across, are borne in thick cylindrical clusters 5 to 15 cm long. There are about 20 stamens and they extend conspicuously beyond the petals. When ripe, in August, the fruit is less than 1 cm in diameter, has become red-purple to black, and is nearly all stone. These small cherries make excellent jelly, pancake syrup, and wine. Most people find the fresh fruits too bitter, but they are relished by songbirds and mammals. Indians used the berries in soups and stews and for mixing with pemmican. Other parts of the plant served several medicinal purposes. Leaves and twigs of the shrub are eaten by deer, elk, and moose.

Saskatoon; Serviceberry

BJKWY

Amelanchier alnifolia

ROSE FAMILY

Saskatoon is a shrub or small bushy tree, 1 to 8 m tall, often spreading by stolons and forming dense colonies. The reddish-brown branches become grey with age. The oval leaves are 2 to 5 cm long, just a little longer than broad, with margins coarsely toothed on the outer half. Fragrant clusters of showy white flowers appear in late May or early June. The 5 petals are linear to oblong and are slightly twisted. When mature, the apple-like fruits, about 1 cm in diameter, become dark purple and are sought by both people and wildlife. They were regarded as the most important vegetable food of the Blackfoot Indians, being used fresh in soups, stews, and pemmican, and being dried for winter. The dried berries were a common article of trade and the wood was prized for making arrows. Today the delicious berries are renowned for making excellent pies and preserves. Bears, chipmunks, squirrels, and a host of birds also relish the fruits. All of the native ungulates are fond of the leaves and twigs. Saskatoon is a common shrub in coulees, bluffs, and open woods.

Chokecherry

Chokecherry

Saskatoon

Saskatoon

False Hellebore

BJKWY

Veratrum viride [*V. eschscholtzii*]

LILY FAMILY

Its great size and beautiful foliage alone make False Hellebore an impressive sight. This robust herb, 1 to 2 m tall, grows from a thick rootstock, which produces only a single stem. The large, prominently ribbed leaves overlap one another up the stem, like shingles on a roof, until the tassels of flowers begin. Individually, the greenish-yellow flowers are disappointing, but massed together on long arching or drooping branches near the top of the spike, they are impressive. The 6-parted, star-shaped flowers have a musky odour. When young, all parts of the plant are highly poisonous to grazing mammals. The dried root was snuffed by some Indians as a remedy for headaches. False Hellebore may be found from low elevation swamps to moist timberline meadows.

Bracted Orchid

BJKWY

Habenaria viridis

ORCHID FAMILY

While its flowers are not strikingly beautiful, this orchid attracts attention by the oddity of the long, tapering bracts which stand out from the flowering spike like little stakes. Among the bracts, and almost hidden by them, are the small, inconspicuous, green flowers. Close examination of a flower reveals a spur and distinctive lip. The lip is spoon-shaped with 2 or 3 prominent teeth at the tip; the spur is about half as long as the lip. Several dark green, oval to lance-shaped leaves ascend the stem, becoming smaller as they merge into the floral spike. Bracted Orchid grows in open woods and moist meadows almost to timberline.

Western Wake Robin

W

Trillium ovatum

LILY FAMILY

Western Wake Robin is a very rare plant in the southern limits of the Canadian Rockies. The common name is a reference to the plant's early blooming, while *Trillium* refers to the 3 leaves, 3 petals, and 3 sepals. Each stem, 20 to 40 cm tall, produces a single, striking white flower that turns pink through purple with age. This flower is regally perched above a ring of 3 broadly ovate leaves, which are sharply tipped. The fruit is a fleshy green pod with winged ridges. This interesting plant favours damp, protected habitats with rich soil.

False Hellebore

Bracted Orchid

Western Wake Robin
*(*Photo courtesy of Simon Lunn*)*

Western Wake Robin

Sweet Coltsfoot BJ

Petasites nivalis [*P. hyperboreus*] COMPOSITE FAMILY

The flowering stems, 30 or 40 cm tall, appear early in the season, well before the triangular- to heart-shaped basal leaves develop. The heads consist of clusters of numerous small, white to purplish flowers. Within a few days the flowers are succeeded by seed-bearing tufts of whitish hairs, not unlike the "puff" of dandelions. After the seeds disperse, the leaves, dark green above and pubescent and whitish beneath, grow from the same fleshy underground rootstock that gave rise to the flowering stems earlier in the season. The leaves are lobed to about one-quarter to one-third of their width. Young leaves and flowers may be eaten raw as salad or cooked as a potherb; dried stems and leaves were used as a salt substitute by Indians. Sweet Coltsfoot grows in moist meadows and along brooks and streams in the alpine and subalpine zones.

White Thistle; Hooker's Thistle BJKWY

Cirsium hookerianum COMPOSITE FAMILY

This stately thistle, 30 to 100 cm tall, is a biennial or short-lived perennial, which grows from a taproot. The alternate leaves, up to 20 cm long, are linear-oblong, lobed or merely toothed, and spine-tipped. They are white and woolly beneath and smooth above. The flower heads are 3 to 5 cm across and there may be a few or several on each plant. Each head has white or creamy white disk florets, sometimes tinged with purple, clustered at the top of the stem. The involucre is shaped like a cup, tipped with spines, and covered with loose, spreading, cobweb-like white hairs. The roots are very tasty and may be eaten raw or cooked with meat. Deer, elk, bears, and horses favour this plant. Preferring moist sites in valley bottoms, White Thistle may be found in bloom during mid- to late summer.

Pearly Everlasting BJKWY

Anaphalis margaritacea COMPOSITE FAMILY

Pearly Everlasting is a perennial, 25 to 30 cm tall, growing from a rhizome. Its lance-shaped leaves are greyish-green on top and white and woolly underneath. At the tip of the stem there is a cluster of many pearly-white flower heads. The pearly effect is due to the whitened tips of papery-thin bracts, which surround the tiny, yellow disk florets. These flowers retain their colour, form, and fresh look for days after being picked, and as a result they are popular in dried arrangements, which makes the common name both appropriate and descriptive. Indians are reported to have placed dried, powdered flowers of this plant on horses' hooves and between their ears to make them long-winded, spirited, and enduring. This plant is fairly common in open woods at low to middle altitudes.

Sweet Coltsfoot

White Thistle

Pearly Everlasting

Pale Comandra; Bastard Toadflax BJKWY

Comandra umbellata [*C. pallida*] SANDALWOOD FAMILY

This erect, blue-green perennial grows from a white, creeping rootstock. Numerous lance-shaped leaves, often delicately flushed with pink, hug the 10 to 30 cm of the stem. The greenish-white sepals are separate above and fused into a small funnel below. There are no petals. The flowers are in rounded or flat-topped clusters at the summit of the stems. Pale Comandra is a parasite that takes its food from the roots of other plants. It is common in open pine woods, prairie grasslands, and on gravelly hillsides.

Northern Bedstraw BJKWY

Galium boreale MADDER FAMILY

Northern Bedstraw is one of our most common roadside and woodland plants. Its dense clusters of tiny, fragrant white flowers are familiar to many. The cross-like flowers, clustered at the tops of stems, each have 4 spreading petals that are joined at the base, but there are no sepals. Each flower produces a 2-parted fruit, splitting into separate bristly achenes at maturity. The smooth stems are square in cross section and bear whorls of 4 narrow, lance-like leaves, each with 3 veins. Some Indians used the roots of this plant to dye porcupine quills red and yellow. As suggested by the common name, the dried, sweet-smelling plants were once used to stuff mattresses.

Poison Ivy W

Rhus radicans SUMAC FAMILY

Poison Ivy is an erect to spreading shrub, up to 40 cm high, which spreads from a creeping rootstock to produce patches of the plant. The leaves consist of 3 large, shiny green leaflets. They are drooping, strongly veined, and pointed, with irregularly notched margins. In the autumn the leaves turn brilliant red. Numerous small, yellowish-green flowers are borne on erect stems. They develop into dull, yellowish, waxy fruits, less than 1 cm in diameter. This plant contains a non-volatile oil, which may cause intense skin irritation when touched. These distressing effects may be reduced by washing with soap and application of ointments. It is better to avoid the plant by remembering the saying, "Leaves 3— let it be." Although generally a rare plant in our region, Poison Ivy may be locally abundant in shady woodlands and ravines.

Pale Comandra

Northern Bedstraw

Poison Ivy

Poison Ivy

Queen's Cup; One-flowered Clintonia; Bluebead Lily JKWY

Clintonia uniflora LILY FAMILY

For simple delicate beauty, Queen's Cup challenges most mountain flowering plants to surpass its charm. The slender stem, about 15 cm tall, bears 1 (occasionally 2) saucer-shaped, 6-pointed, pure white flower with a crown of golden anthers. The plant has 2 or 3 large, glossy green basal leaves. Both the stems and leaves are clothed with fine white hairs. The short-lived flower is succeeded by a shiny, deep blue, bead-like berry, which in its own way is as elegant as the blossom it replaced. This attractive lily prefers a mossy habitat in the shade of coniferous forests.

Death Camas BKW

Zigadenus [*Zygadenus*] *venenosus* [*Z. gramineus*] LILY FAMILY

Death Camas is of considerable interest and charm without being spectacular in any way. Its narrow, green, grass-like leaves, sheathing at the base, form loose tufts from which rise 20- to 40-cm stems carrying racemes of creamy flowers. This plant can be distinguished from White Camas by its much more compact spike of smaller flowers. The onion-like bulb is extremely poisonous, especially to sheep. These bulbs were sometimes confused by Indians and early settlers, often with deadly results, with those of Blue Camas, a staple spring food. For that reason the plants were regularly dug out and destroyed in some of the favourite camas-gathering areas. Mashed bulbs of this plant were used as an external cure for boils and rheumatism and in easing pain caused by bruises and sprains. Flowering in the early summer, Death Camas is a fairly common plant on prairies and moist meadows.

White Camas; Mountain Death Camas BJKWY

Zigadenus [*Zygadenus*] *elegans* LILY FAMILY

This handsome plant, from 30 to 60 cm tall, grows from a blackish-coated bulb 7 to 15 cm below the ground surface. Its V-shaped, smooth, grass-like leaves are slightly curved lengthwise and somewhat bluish-green in colour. The stems are slender, often pinkish, and terminate in a graceful spray of dainty greenish- to yellowish-white flowers. These 6-parted flowers are 1 or 2 cm across, and both sepals and petals have round, greenish glands near the base. Though an attractive plant to look at, the flowers smell foul. The mature capsule has 3 lobes and many seeds. Like other members of this genus, White Camas contains an alkaloid and all parts can be poisonous to humans and grazing animals. White Camas may be found in open meadows from low elevations to alpine areas.

Queen's Cup

Queen's Cup

Death Camas

White Camas

Alpine Smelowskia; Silver Rockcress — BJW

Smelowskia calycina — MUSTARD FAMILY

This densely tufted perennial is widespread on scree slopes and rocky crests at high elevations. The blue-grey basal leaves may be lance-shaped or deeply cleft into several lobes; stem leaves are smaller and finely dissected. Both leaves and stems are fringed with hairs. Short racemes of creamy white flowers bloom at the stem tips, but these racemes elongate as the fruits develop. The resulting pods are dark-coloured, slender, and pointed at both ends. Alpine Smelowskia is often infected by an invading rust fungus whose mycelium extracts food from the host plant and, in the process, causes flower abortion and disfiguration of leaves. The rust becomes evident on the leaves and stems as numerous brown, pimple-like protuberances which soon become powdery.

Viviparous Knotweed; Alpine Bistort — BJKWY

Polygonum viviparum — BUCKWHEAT FAMILY

A slender, unbranched perennial, 10 to 13 cm tall, Viviparous Knotweed grows from a starchy, edible rootstock. There is a cluster of petioled basal leaves, which are lance-shaped, dark green, and shiny. Stem leaves are few and small in size. White or pink flowers with protruding, fuzzy-looking stamens cluster on the stem. *Viviparum* means "to bring forth live young" and refers to the tiny, pinkish-purple bulblets on the lower part of the stem, each capable of producing a new plant while still attached to the parent. The rootstocks may be eaten raw or cooked, and are said to taste like almonds. Leaves may be included in salads or cooked as a potherb. A yellow dye can be produced from the stem. Viviparous Knotweed is a common plant in alpine meadows and at the margins of lakes and streams.

White Draba; White Whitlow Grass — BJKWY

Draba lonchocarpa — MUSTARD FAMILY

The drabas, or whitlow grasses, have cross-like flowers each with 4 sepals and 4 petals. In addition, they have 6 stamens, 2 being shorter than the others and on opposite sides of the pistil. Identification at the species level affords many difficult problems for flower lovers as well as expert botanists. Seed pod and hair-type characteristics must often be studied for certain determination. This particular species is a dwarf, matted plant less than 8 cm high. It has small hairy leaves and clusters of tiny white flowers set on top of a short stem. Rocky areas and scree slopes are favoured habitats.

Alpine Smelowskia

Alpine Smelowskia, rust-infected

Viviparous Knotweed

White Draba

Red-stemmed Saxifrage BJKWY

Saxifraga lyallii SAXIFRAGE FAMILY

Red-stemmed saxifrage is usually found embedded in mosses that border small stream banks in alpine and subalpine regions. The purple-coloured stems, 10 to 30 cm tall, each bearing 1 to several tiny, white, star-shaped flowers, contrast prettily with their mossy surroundings. At maturity the sepals are reflexed and the white petals are marked with 2 greenish-yellow blotches that later fade. Brownish, 3-pointed, erect capsules later replace the flowers. The leaves of this plant are coarsely toothed and fan-shaped, growing in clumps from a long rootstock.

Spotted Saxifrage; Prickly Saxifrage BJKWY

Saxifraga bronchialis SAXIFRAGE FAMILY

This densely matted or cushion-like plant has small leathery, lance-like leaves, overlapping each other. They are fringed with long hairs and each terminates in a sharp spine. The stiffly erect, dark brown flowering stems support a few small leaves and a number of branches. There are numerous star-shaped flowers, which are borne on a flat-topped cluster about 15 cm above the mat of evergreen leaves. The 5 white petals are speckled with purple, orange, or yellow spots so small that the beauty of this flower can best be appreciated only if the admirer gets down on hands and knees. Spotted Saxifrage is a common inhabitant of rock crevices and scree slopes from mid to high elevations.

Wedge-Leaf Saxifrage BJKWY

Saxifraga adscendens SAXIFRAGE FAMILY

This very small alpine plant, growing along mossy brooks or below snowbeds, often escapes notice. It may flower when less than 2 cm tall and the mature stems are not more than 8 cm high. The reddish basal leaves, growing in a dense rosette, are wedge-shaped, as the common name implies, with the narrow portion at the point of attachment. The broad end may be entire or with 3 lobes, the middle one usually the largest. There are usually several smaller leaves along the stem. The small bell-shaped flowers have white, green-veined petals, which are about twice as long as the reddish-purple sepals. All green parts of the plant are glandular and hairy.

Bishop's Cap; Bare-stemmed Mitrewort BJKWY

Mitella nuda SAXIFRAGE FAMILY

The creeping rhizomes of Bishop's Cap give rise to basal clusters of long-petioled, kidney- to heart-shaped leaves with crinkly, toothed margins and erect flowering stems. Reaching a height of 20 or 30 cm, the stems are leafless, with a few yellowish-green flowers resembling tiny pinwheels. To appreciate the superb beauty of the small flower, you may like to examine it with the aid of a hand lens. The 5 petals are delicately fringed threads strung between the unbranched sepals and the 10 stamens, like finely crafted jewels. When opened, the 2-valved capsule contains tiny, shiny, black seeds, not unlike a miniature nest with a clutch of eggs. This dainty beauty is widespread in moist, shaded spruce forests.

Red-stemmed Saxifrage

Spotted Saxifrage

Wedge-leaf Saxifrage

Bishop's Cap

Wind Flower; Cut-leaved Anemone — BJKWY

Anemone multifida — BUTTERCUP FAMILY

Like all anemones, Wind Flower possesses no petals, only sepals. But the sepals display a joyous array of colours ranging from white, yellowish, or red on the inside to bluish or reddish on the outside. These varied hues are complemented by deeply divided, feathery, basal leaves and a collar of 3 stem leaves. Leaves, petioles, and flowering stems are densely hairy. The 5 to 10 blunt-tipped sepals give way to a seedhead of woolly achenes. Wind Flower is wide ranging, from dry grassy slopes to lowland and alpine meadows. It blooms from late May through July.

One-sided Wintergreen — BJKWY

Orthilia secunda [*Pyrola secunda*] — WINTERGREEN FAMILY

This plant grows from long creeping rootstocks and often forms dense colonies in coniferous forests. Its one-sided arrangement of blossoms on the flowering stalk and lantern-shaped, greenish-white flowers are unmistakable. The many flowers are all arranged on the upper part of the stem, which bends gracefully downward, seemingly from their weight. Each flower has a long style with a knob-like tip that projects beyond the corolla and still is evident when the capsule forms. The flowering stem straightens as the many-seeded capsules mature. One-sided Wintergreen leaves are olive-green, variable in shape, and have finely toothed margins. They retain their colour throughout the winter, as suggested by the common name.

One-flowered Wintergreen; Single Delight — BJKWY

Moneses uniflora — WINTERGREEN FAMILY

Less than 10 cm tall, this small perennial has a basal rosette of rounded, veiny, and shallowly toothed leaves. Each leafless stalk supports one winsome nodding flower with ivory-white petals, 10 greenish stamens, and a conspicuous long style extending from the centre. Note the wavy petal margins. It is worth getting down on your hands and knees to discover the lovely fragrance of the flower. Although the flower nods while in bloom, the fruit lengthens and straightens to an upright brown capsule when mature. This delightful, large-flowered plant grows in mossy carpets within coniferous forests.

Wind Flower

One-sided Wintergreen

One-flowered Wintergreen

Mountain Marsh Marigold BJK

Caltha leptosepala BUTTERCUP FAMILY

These white flowers, commonly tinged with blue on the back, brighten marshes, stream banks, and seepage slopes below melting snowbanks near timberline. Each flower is composed of 5 to 10 petal-like segments that appear at the end of a smooth, hollow, pinkish stem. The open flower measures up to 4 cm across and has a bright yellow centre composed of stamens and pistils. A perennial, the plant has soft green, somewhat fleshy, heart-shaped leaves, mostly at the base of the stem. The seeds are borne in top-shaped clusters of papery pods. Despite its harmless appearance, this plant is known to be poisonous to livestock.

Western Canada Violet BJKWY

Viola canadensis [*V. rugulosa*] VIOLET FAMILY

Western Canada Violet is a charming little flower known to many as the trumpeter of early spring. The petals are white to violet, with yellow at the base. Distinctive purple lines that converge on the lower petals guide bees and other insects to the sweet nectar within. The slender stems have several heart-shaped leaves, which form a suitable background for the subtly fragrant flowers. When the seed pods ripen they open with a sudden twist that shoots the seeds some distance away, a habit which reduces competition by the seedling with the parent plant for space, nutrients, and moisture. The leaves and flowers may be eaten raw in salads, boiled as potherbs, or used to thicken soup. The flowers can be candied for use as cake decorations. Western Canada Violet is often found in dense colonies in rich, moist aspen forests.

Kidney-leaved Violet BJKY

Viola renifolia VIOLET FAMILY

Blooming against a background of last year's brown foliage, the familiar blossoms of Kidney-leaved Violet are a welcome sign of the arrival of spring. Individual small white flowers, with the lower petal often streaked with purplish veins, arise on slender leafless stems from a fleshy rootstock. The kidney-shaped leaves have blunt tips and their margins are wavy and toothed. The long, purplish seed capsules split open when ripe, expelling the brown seeds. Like other violets, both the flowers and leaves are edible and the leaves are a good source of vitamins A and C. This small violet may be found in damp shaded woodlands and meadows.

Mountain Marsh Marigold

Western Canada Violet

Kidney-leaved Violet

Bear Grass W

Xerophyllum tenax LILY FAMILY

Once seen, Bear Grass's torch-like cluster of hundreds of small creamy white flowers rising from the large tuft of stiff, grass-like leaves will not be forgotten. A dense basal clump of sharp-edged evergreen leaves, 40 or 50 cm long, rises from a thick rootstock. The spectacular stem, unbranched for the 50 to 120 cm of its length, is covered with shorter needle-like leaves and holds aloft the great plume of flowers, each of which is a miniature lily. The lowermost flowers are the first to open. Position of the flowers varies with the stage of growth: in bud they are pressed to the stem; in bloom they stand out at a sharp angle; and in fruit they are again erect along the stem. Some flower stalks exhibit knee-like curves; these are thought to occur during long rainy periods when the head is bowed down and the stalk matures in that position. Individual plants may be sterile for several years, with flowers present only 1 to 3 times in a 10-year period. Indians are reported to have used the leaves for weaving hats, capes, and baskets. Rocky Mountain goats eat the mature leaves, bears the softer leaf bases in the early spring, and bighorn sheep, deer, and elk feed on the flower clusters and stems. Bear Grass is common on dry hillsides and subalpine meadows in Waterton Lakes National Park, the only Canadian national park in which it occurs.

Red Elderberry BJKWY

Sambucus racemosa HONEYSUCKLE FAMILY

Red Elderberry is a conspicuous shrub up to 3 m tall, often growing in large clumps. It has fast-growing, pithy, partly hollow stems. Each large compound leaf consists of 5 to 7 sawtooth-edged leaflets. The cone-shaped terminal clusters of small, creamy white flowers, held erect like torches, are strongly and sweetly scented. This plant's charm is prolonged by bright scarlet berries that glow where the flowers once bloomed. A multitude of birds feast on the berries, and deer, elk, and moose browse this shrub heavily. The berries are used for making jelly and wine. Both the roots and stems are poisonous; children have been poisoned when stems were hollowed out and used as blowguns. Red Elderberry inhabits stream banks, moist woods, and thickets.

Bear Grass

Bear Grass

Red Elderberry

Red Elderberry

White Geranium

BJKWY

Geranium richardsonii

GERANIUM FAMILY

White Geranium, 30 to 80 cm high, is one of the most appealing plants found in aspen glades along the lower slopes of the mountains. The open, gleaming white petals, often with pink or purple veins, are accentuated by the shapely leaves. The long-petioled, opposite leaves are sparsely hairy, deeply lobed, and split into between 3 and 7 toothed divisions. When ripe, the long-beaked capsule splits into 5 portions lengthways from the bottom, and does so with enough force to catapult the seeds some distance from the parent plant, thus reducing competition with future generations of geraniums.

Mountain Fleabane

BJKWY

Erigeron humilis

COMPOSITE FAMILY

Another charming little plant of moist alpine slopes, Mountain Fleabane is seldom more than 15 cm tall. The plant grows from a taproot and produces stems which are more or less erect. Each stem is crowned with a solitary flower head with 50 to 150 white ray flowers that age to a light purple. The basal leaves are spoon-shaped, tapering into long petioles. Long hairs are present on all green parts of the plant; those on the involucral bracts and adjacent stem are woolly and blackish-purple. Fruits are yellow-ribbed and hairy, with white pappus bristles.

White Dryad; White Mountain Avens

BJKWY

Dryas octopetala

ROSE FAMILY

White Dryad is one of the most abundant and attractive flowers of the alpine zone. It grows close to the ground, forming an evergreen mat in gravelly or stony dry places, and it blooms soon after the snow melts. Numerous creamy flowers, with many yellow stamens, are contrasted against the low mat of leaves. The flowering stems rise 6 to 16 cm above the matted leaves, depending on the degree of protection from the elements. Each flower has 8 petals, hence the name *octopetala*. As with the Yellow Dryad, the persistent styles lengthen into long feathery tails that serve as parachutes in spreading of the seeds. The rough-surfaced, leathery leaves have scalloped edges and are dark green above, with the underside coated by dense white hairs. White Dryad is superbly adapted to its rigorous environment. For example, the deeply anchored root and leathery leaves help the plant withstand winds at high elevations, while root-nodules store nitrogen in a habitat where nutrients are generally washed out of the soil by melting snow. Both the blooms and the seed plumes are reported to produce a vivid green dye.

White Geranium

Mountain Fleabane

White Dryad

Water Hemlock

BJKW

Cicuta maculata [*C. douglasii*]

PARSNIP FAMILY

Among the most deadly poisonous plants of the continent, Water Hemlock is fairly common along slough margins, lakeshores, and other wet areas. This stout-stemmed plant, from 50 to 200 cm tall, grows from a thick tuberous root which is divided horizontally into several chambers. Even a small piece of the root would contain enough poison, primarily the alkaloid coniine, to kill humans and livestock. The leaves are alternate and pinnately compound, with sharply toothed leaflets, and they vary in size up the stem. Rounded compound umbels, up to 10 cm wide, consisting of numerous small white flowers, rise from the tip of the stem. Secondary umbels grow from several narrow bracts. The oval-shaped seeds are yellow with dark brown ribs.

False Asphodel

BJKWY

Tofieldia glutinosa

LILY FAMILY

A distinctive feature of this plant is the upper portion of the flowering stem, which is glandular and sticky. White flowers are clustered at the tips of the stems, their dark anthers conspicuous against the white of the petals. Erect, plump, reddish seed capsules develop after the flowers fade. The 3 or 4 leaves are basal and grass-like and about half the length of the stems. Search for False Asphodel along the edges of open bogs or ponds. Bog Asphodel (*T. pusilla*) grows in similar habitats; its stems are thinner and are not sticky.

False Solomon's Seal; False Spikenard

BJKWY

Smilacina racemosa

LILY FAMILY

False Solomon's Seal has arching or erect stems up to 1 m tall that arise from a fleshy underground stem. The large, sharply pointed, oval to broadly lance-shaped leaves either clasp around the stem or are attached by short petioles. These prominently veined leaves are a handsome setting for the terminal cluster of many minute white flowers. The flowers have long stamens and a redolent fragrance. Pea-sized, bright red berries, often dotted with purple, mature later in the season. This lovely plant is common in moist, shaded woodland habitats.

Water Hemlock

False Asphodel

False Solomon's Seal

Western Meadow Rue BJKWY

Thalictrum occidentale BUTTERCUP FAMILY

This is a dioecious species, which means that male and female flowers are found on separate plants. Male flowers are greenish-purple with clusters of drooping stamens; female flowers are greenish-white with 8 to 15 tiny pistils. There are no petals on the tassel-like flowers and the sepals are numerous but not conspicuous. The gracefully formed leaves are the plant's chief attraction. The stems, 30 to 100 cm tall, bear large bluish-green, prominently veined, compound leaves, which are divided 2 or 3 times into delicate, fan-shaped leaflets. Juice from this plant is acrid and bitter. Its roots were a source of yellow dye. The seed and foliage were used by Indians as a perfume and perhaps as an insect repellant. Powdered foliage of the plant was given to horses as a tonic. Western Meadow Rue is common and widely distributed in moist woods, thickets, meadows, and along streams.

Blunt-leaved Bog Orchid; Small Northern Bog Orchid BJKWY

Habenaria obtusata [*Platanthera obtusata*] ORCHID FAMILY

This humble little orchid is easily identified by its single, broadly blunted, clasping leaf. The stem is between 10 and 20 cm tall and bears a succession of uncrowded greenish-white flowers, usually fewer than 10. A distinctive hood, formed by the 2 lateral petals and the sepals, overhangs the narrow, strap-shaped lip like a flat-topped porch. The spur is tapered and curves slightly downward. Mosquitoes, with a selective taste for the nectar of this plant, are important in its cross-pollination. Blunt-leaved Bog Orchid grows in the damp cool soils of bogs, mossy stream banks, and dense coniferous forests.

Northwest Twayblade BJW

Listera caurina ORCHID FAMILY

A litter of needles under a cool coniferous forest is the favoured habitat of Northwest Twayblade. From 15 to 23 cm tall, the stem has a pair of leaves opposite one another about midway along its length. These egg-shaped leaves are noticeably roughened by numerous small glands. Tiny greenish-yellow flowers, with widely spreading sepals and petals, are in a loosely spaced raceme. The flower has a rounded lip at the tip and a pair of peculiar rounded swellings at the base, which are best inspected with a magnifying glass. A pair of horn-like appendages spreads from these swellings.

Western Meadow Rue—male

Western Meadow Rue—female

Blunt-leaved Bog Orchid

Northwest Twayblade

Thimbleberry; Salmonberry

JKWY

Rubus parviflorus

ROSE FAMILY

Unlike the closely related raspberry, this vigorous shrub does not have prickles or spines. Between 50 and 200 cm tall, it has large leaves, each with 3 or 5 lobes and with jagged-toothed margins. These rich green, maple-like leaves enhance the background for the attractive white blooms with their central boss of golden stamens. There are usually 3 to 5 flowers in clusters at the ends of the branches. The bright red fruit, which looks like a flat raspberry, is edible but rather tasteless and very seedy. Thimbleberry often forms thickets on avalanche slopes and along the margins of forests.

Common Yarrow; Milfoil

BJKWY

Achillea millefolium

COMPOSITE FAMILY

This genus is named in honour of Achilles, the Greek warrior with the vulnerable heel, who was said to have made an ointment from Yarrow to heal the wounds of his soldiers during the siege of Troy. The stems of this aromatic perennial arise from a creeping rootstock and may be 20 to 70 cm tall. The flat-topped cluster of small blooms consists of two kinds of flowers. The white (rarely pink) ray florets ringing each cluster have a 2-notched lip at the top of the tube, whereas the tube of the straw-coloured disk florets is evenly notched with 5 short teeth. A leaf, or foil, may not be divided a thousand times as the scientific name (*millefolium*) implies, but it is very much dissected. Before flowering, Common Yarrow may be mistaken for a fern because of the lacy, much-divided leaves. These attractive plants are frequently used in dried arrangements. It is reported that the Indians used the plant to treat cuts and open wounds, as a tonic, and as a cure for stomach disorders. Common Yarrow is equally at home anywhere from the grasslands to mountain summits.

Common Labrador Tea

BJKY

Ledum groenlandicum

HEATH FAMILY

Common Labrador Tea is a much-branched, aromatic evergreen shrub, 30 to 80 cm tall, that grows in mossy bogs and moist coniferous woods. Its leaves are a distinguishing feature. They are narrowly oblong, thick and leathery, dark glossy green above and rusty and woolly beneath, with downward-rolled margins. Numerous small white flowers, with stamens that rise from the centre of each bloom, are clustered at hairy branch-tips. The stalks are erect when in flower but drooping in fruit, which is a 5-valved capsule containing many seeds. When crushed the leaves have a spicy aroma, redolent with the tang of the moist woods and bogs in which they grow. Ledol, a toxic compound, and narcotic substances are found in the leaves. However, the leaves have long been used as a substitute or additive for tea, and those substances may produce restorative effects similar to those resulting from caffeine. Several medicinal uses are reported, including relief of dysentery and promotion of digestion. The Indians extracted oil to use for tanning skins and as a lotion to relieve the itch of insect bites.

Thimbleberry

Thimbleberry

Common Yarrow

Common Labrador Tea

Franklin's Lady's Slipper; Sparrow's-Egg Lady's Slipper

BJKWY

Cypripedium passerinum

ORCHARD FAMILY

This small-flowered plant was given the name *passerinum*, meaning "sparrow-like," because the flower forms an inflated and sac-like pouch that is spotted like a sparrow's egg and about the same shape and size. The pouch is white, rarely pink, with bright purple dots on the interior. The sepals are short, stubby, and greenish in colour. The stems, which are 15 to 25 cm tall, grow from a fibrous rootstock and have large, prominently veined, clasping leaves. Both stems and leaves are covered with soft hairs. This little gem will be found in deep mossy coniferous forests, on gravel outwashes, and on the borders of ponds and streams. Picking this flower is particularly destructive: the flower quickly wilts, while the plant dies.

Mountain Lady's Slipper

KW

Cypripedium montanum

ORCHID FAMILY

Among the showiest of orchids in the Canadian Rockies, Mountain Lady's Slipper occurs in open woods. This mountain relative of Yellow Lady's Slipper is rarer and much less widely distributed. Rising from a cord-like rhizome, the stems bear 4 to 6 hairy leaves. These lance-shaped leaves clasp the stem and have numerous parallel veins which converge at the pointed tips. At the top of the stem, up to 3 widely spreading, delightfully scented flowers develop. Both the sepals and petals are richly marked with brown. The thin, pointed petals are spirally twisted. The lip is the most distinctive feature of the flower, being a luminous white slipper or pouch, delicately veined at the base with purple. There are also colourful spots of purple within the slipper and a yellow tongue extends outward from above the slipper's opening.

Round-leaved Orchid

BJKWY

Orchis rotundifolia

ORCHID FAMILY

This exquisite orchid arises from thick, fleshy roots in bogs and moist, cool coniferous woods. A single elliptic or oval leaf cradles a slender, leafless stem 10 to 25 cm high. Commonly, 3 to 8 flowers are spaced along the upper end of the stem. A distinguishing feature of this flower is the white, tongue-like lip, speckled with minute dots of magenta. The lip is 3-lobed, the middle lobe being the largest and having a notch at the end. It is covered by a rose- to white-coloured bonnet formed by the sepals and 2 lateral petals. The spur is stout and slightly curved.

Franklin's Lady's Slipper

Mountain Lady's Slipper

Round-leaved Orchid

Low Bush Cranberry; Mooseberry BJKWY

Viburnum edule HONEYSUCKLE FAMILY

Until the brilliant scarlet fruits are framed in a mat of snow or the maple-like leaves turn to crimson-purple, this common shrub of the woodlands tends to get overlooked. It is a straggly shrub, 1 to 2 m tall, whose mature leaves are maple-shaped while younger leaves are pointed and lance-shaped. The tiny, white, 5-parted flowers are arranged in flat-topped showy clusters between pairs of leaves along the stem. The fruits are juicy and acidic and contain a large, flattened stone. They hang on the tree after the leaves fall, providing a valuable food source for birds. Frequently the fruit ferments on the shrubs, resulting in many a tipsy bird. In addition to being favoured by birds, these edible fruits make a tasty, tart jelly. The fruits also have a delicate fragrance, which wafts through the air on pleasant autumn days.

White Water Crowfoot BWY

Ranunculus aquatilis BUTTERCUP FAMILY

Bright little white flowers, often flecked with gold at the base, are buoyed above the water surface on short stalks. This aquatic buttercup has 2 types of leaves. The submerged ones are divided into thread-like filaments while the few floating ones, when present, are deeply cleft into 3 to 5 lobes. In addition to the yellow flecks at the base of the petals, numerous stamens and pistils attract insects which pollinate the flowers. White Water Crowfoot sometimes entirely covers shallow ponds, lakes, ditches, and streams with its showy blossoms.

Low Bush Cranberry

Low Bush Cranberry

White Water Crowfoot

Yellow Hedysarum — BKWY

Hedysarum sulphurescens — PEA FAMILY

Yellow Hedysarum is a herb 30 to 60 cm tall, usually with a single erect stem growing from a stout, somewhat woody, perennial rootstock. Its leaves consist of 9 to 17 leaflets, which have obvious veins. The small, creamy white flowers are in a rather open cluster at the end of a stalk which arises from the upper leaf axils. Drooping seed pods, about 2.5 cm long, replace the flowers. As with Northern Sweetvetch, the constrictions between each seed in the pod easily distinguish this hedysarum from milkvetches and locoweeds, whose flowers may look similar but whose pods are shaped more like those of garden peas. This unmistakable plant grows in dense clumps along stream banks, in moist woods, and occasionally in alpine sites. It is a very important food plant for grizzly bears, which eat the roots in spring and fall.

Rattlesnake Plantain — BJKWY

Goodyera oblongifolia — ORCHID FAMILY

As the species name implies, the evergreen basal leaves are oblong. They are quite striking, with a blue-green colour and a broad white stripe down the centre, sometimes with a whitish net-like pattern of veins extending beyond the middle of the blade. The robust downy spike is 20 to 35 cm tall, and bears from 10 to 30 small flowers in a loose one-sided raceme. These flowers are a drab greenish-white. The lip has a wide-open mouth pressed up almost against the overhanging hood. Look for Rattlesnake Plantain in coniferous forests at low elevations, where it usually flowers in August.

Umbrella Plant; Wild Buckwheat — BJKWY

Eriogonum umbellatum [*E. subalpinum*] — BUCKWHEAT FAMILY

Umbrella Plant is a perennial that grows from 10 to 30 cm tall. Its basal leaves, though variable in shape, are generally lance- to spoon-shaped. They are densely covered with white hairs beneath, but have a green upper surface. The stem leaves occur in a whorl at the top of the main stem where it is divided into 6 or more smaller stalks, creating the flower umbels. The umbrella-like clusters of flowers are greenish-white to pale sulphur-yellow, often flecked with a faintly rose flush as they age. Reportedly, the leaves may be boiled to make tea. This plant is widely distributed on exposed sites from low elevations to alpine ridges.

Yellow Hedysarum

Yellow Hedysarum

Rattlesnake Plantain

Umbrella Plant

Woolly Fleabane BJKW

Erigeron lanatus COMPOSITE FAMILY

A squat perennial growing on rocky slopes in high alpine areas, Woolly Fleabane is anchored by long taproots and has short stems, seldom over 10 cm tall. The small leaves, in a basal rosette, are rounded at the apex and often 3-toothed. Up to nearly 3 cm in diameter, the daisy-like head has numerous and unusually long ray flowers, which are normally white but occasionally a pale lilac. Disk flowers are yellow. Upper portions of the involucral bracts and upper stems are a dark purple. Loose, branching hairs entirely cover the leaves, stems, and involucral bracts; this densely woolly covering gives the plant its common and species names. Fruits are dry achenes with white bristles.

Low Townsendia BJKW

Townsendia hookeri [*T. sericea, T. exscapa*] COMPOSITE FAMILY

Low Townsendia is an almost stemless plant growing from a deep woody root. Stalkless flower heads are borne among a rosette of lance-shaped leaves, which are sharply pointed and covered with fine, silvery hairs. White to pink ray flowers surround the yellow disk flowers. The involucral bracts have a green midrib and most have white margin hairs. This plant may be expected on prairies and dry hillsides, but it is conspicuous only when flowering in the early spring.

Daisy Fleabane; Cutleaf Fleabane BJKWY

Erigeron compositus COMPOSITE FAMILY

The pretty daisy-like blossoms of this fleabane usually have ray flowers that are white, pink, or mauve. The many disk flowers are yellow. Several stems arise from the base, each crowned with a single flower head. Except for a few reduced bracts on the stem, the foliage is almost entirely comprised of deeply divided basal leaves. Both the leaves and stems are sparsely covered with short glandular hairs. The involucral bracts, as seen in the photograph, are also hairy and purplish, at least at the tips. Daisy Fleabane grows in rocky soils from moderate elevations to the alpine zone.

Woolly Fleabane

Low Townsendia

Daisy Fleabane

Indian Paintbrush

BJKWY

Castilleja species

FIGWORT FAMILY

Indian Paintbrush is one of the most abundant and variable plants within the Canadian Rockies. The colour of the "brush" is not due to the flowers, which are narrow, tubular, and greenish-yellow, but to the floral bracts which enfold them. These bracts may be brilliant blood-red, delicate pink, orange, or occasionally even yellow or white. The stems, 10 to 60 cm tall, often form large clumps. There are numerous alternate leaves, linear to elliptic in shape, each having 3 prominent parallel veins. The much-branched rootstock is a root-parasite which makes transplanting the paintbrush to a home garden almost impossible. There are at least 10 species of paintbrushes in the southern Canadian Rocky Mountains. Their identification can be frustrating even for botanical experts. The many hues of the paintbrushes dominate well-drained slopes and rocky ledges, from low elevations to alpine meadows.

Indian Paintbrush

Indian Paintbrush

Indian Paintbrush

Indian Paintbrush

Red and White Baneberry BJKWY

Actaea rubra BUTTERCUP FAMILY

This perennial herb, 50 to 100 cm tall, is better known for its berries than for its flowers. Scores of very small flowers, with 3 to 5 white petal-like sepals and 5 to 10 white petals, form a rounded cluster on an elongated stalk. Neither sepals nor petals remain for long, and they fall at the slightest touch. The conspicuous fruits, about the size of a pea, come in two colour phases, a lustrous coral-red and a startling ivory-white. These fruits are surrounded by large handsome leaves; they are thin, delicate, and 3-parted with many deeply saw-toothed, pointed leaflets. All parts of the plant, including the berries, contain a poisonous compound. The roots are reported to have been boiled by Indians and the decoction taken for coughs and colds or used to treat sick horses. This woodland dweller may be found in moist coniferous forests.

Silver-leaved Scorpionweed KWY

Phacelia hastata [*P. heterophylla, P. leptosepala*] WATERLEAF FAMILY

This densely hairy perennial grows from a stout rootstock, producing stems 15 to 40 cm high. The leaves are smooth-margined and lance-shaped, with conspicuous lateral veins that converge toward the tip. As suggested by the common name, they appear a dull grey, being covered with both dense, fine, fuzzy hairs and long, flattened, coarse hairs. Numerous flowers in separate dense clusters are located at the top of each branching stem. Although mostly cream-coloured to nearly white, the flowers may occasionally be pinkish or bluish. The filaments usually are bearded, protruding out of the flower. Silver-leaved Scorpionweed is common on dry, exposed rocky slopes at middle elevations.

Western Spring Beauty BJKWY

Claytonia lanceolata PURSLANE FAMILY

These attractive and abundant plants grow from small underground corms about 2 cm in diameter. The plants have several green to reddish stems with 2 opposite lance-shaped leaves on each. From 3 to 15 flowers, clustered on a one-sided raceme, bloom above the succulent leaves. Each flower has 5 petals, cupped in 2 sepals. Slightly notched at the top, the petals are white to pink in colour and attractively streaked with rose or purple veins which join at the base. As suggested by its name, this is one of the earliest flowers to bloom, sprouting as early as late April beside the snowbanks retreating from the valley floor, though it will not be seen on alpine slopes until July. The dense mounds of emerald-green leaves and star-shaped flowers are soon concealed by the vigorous growth of other herbs and grasses. The corms used to be dug in the spring by Indians and were eaten as we would potatoes. These buried treasures, as evidenced by numerous diggings, are known to grizzly bears and other, smaller animals as well.

Red and White Baneberry

Red and White Baneberry

Silver-leaved Scorpionweed

Western Spring Beauty

Clustered Oreocarya

W

Cryptantha nubigena

BORAGE FAMILY

All green parts of Clustered Oreocarya are densely covered with rather bristly white hairs, often giving it a grey appearance. The somewhat spoon-shaped lower leaves have rounded or sharp tips, while the upper leaves are linear. Small flowers cluster in the axils of the leaves over the upper two-thirds of the stem. The flowers, showy white with yellow centres, have a sweet perfume. The calyx is very bristly, and the nutlet is ridged on the back. This plant grows on dry hillsides and prairies, sometimes densely.

Bladder Campion

BWY

Silene cucubalus

PINK FAMILY

An introduced perennial weed, Bladder Campion has deep roots that allow it to survive on roadsides, in gravel pits, and in other disturbed places. A conspicuous feature of the plant is an inflated sepal tube, marked by a network of darker veins. The corolla is formed by 5 deeply bilobed petals, which spread out like a wheel just beyond the rim of the sepal tube. The stems may be up to 1 m tall and branched from the base, the lower branches sometimes spreading horizontally before ascending. The opposite, lance-shaped leaves are produced from swollen leaf nodes. This rapidly spreading plant may crowd out some desirable native species.

Long-stalked Chickweed

BJKWY

Stellaria monantha [*S. longipes* var. *altocaulis*]

PINK FAMILY

Long-stalked Chickweed is a tufted perennial with blue-green, lance-shaped leaves, which are sessile and opposite. Its stems, flowers, and leaves are generally rigidly erect, in contrast to several other Chickweeds. The white flowers may be solitary at the end of the straight stalks or with 1 or more flowers from branches at the leaf axils below the terminal flower. There are only 5 petals, but they are so deeply cleft there appear to be 10. This plant inhabits exposed rocky ridges and slopes within the alpine zone. The young leaves of the plant may be chopped and eaten raw or cooked. They are rich sources of vitamin C and iron. Several species of Chickweed are found in the Canadian Rocky Mountains. They are not always easily identified because they tend to be highly variable.

Mountain Chickweed

BJKWY

Cerastium beeringianum

PINK FAMILY

Another delightful little plant of exposed alpine ridges, Mountain Chickweed is of low stature and often forms matted clumps. The stems are 5 to 25 cm tall, hairy, and sticky. The cheery white flowers have 5 petals, each with a prominent cleft at the tip. Smaller than the petals, the sepals have translucent margins and are often tinged with purple. The sessile leaves, covered with silky hairs, are said to resemble mouse ears. When fully mature the fruit is a cylindrical capsule.

Clustered Oreocarya

Bladder Campion

Long-stalked Chickweed

Mountain Chickweed

Clasping-leaved Twisted Stalk

BJKWY

Streptopus amplexifolius

LILY FAMILY

This plant has a widely branching zigzag stem. Numerous sharply pointed, parallel-veined leaves encircle the stem at each angular bend. These graceful, glossy leaves often conceal the 1 or 2 dainty little flowers dangling on curving thread-like stalks from the axil of each of the upper leaves. Each greenish-yellow flower has strongly reflexed petals and sepals. Shiny orange or red berries, which are oblong and contain numerous seeds, replace the flowers. Clasping-leaved Twisted Stalk favours moist, shaded forests at middle elevations.

Few-flowered Anemone; Northern Anemone

BJKWY

Anemone parviflora

BUTTERCUP FAMILY

Few-flowered Anemone prefers moist soils from lowland floodplains to stream banks above timberline. The stalk is 15 to 30 cm tall and supports a single flower. The flower has 5 or 6 creamy white sepals, which are always hairy and usually tinged with blue-purple on the back. The oval-shaped fruiting cluster is covered by dense, white, woolly hair. The basal leaves are few in number, long-petioled and divided into 3 leaflets, which are cleft about halfway and have blunt teeth on the margins. Bracts on the elongating stalk have 3 lobes and are deeply cleft. Depending on the altitude, the plant may flower from June through August.

White-flowered Rhododendron

BJKWY

Rhododendron albiflorum

HEATH FAMILY

Of all shrubs that inhabit the cool, moist, mature montane and subalpine forests, White-flowered Rhododendron, a deciduous bush, has one of the largest flowers, 2 or 3 cm across. These white to cream-white flowers are shaped like a cup, with the petals joined to one another for about half of their length. There are 10 pale yellow stamens, hairy at their bases. The flowers, produced singly or in clusters of 2 or 3, are borne on branches of the previous season's growth. The calyx is deciduous as a unit with the corolla, so the forest floor may be covered with what looks like intact white flowers. Tufts of rather thin, lance-shaped leaves, shiny green above and paler beneath, with smooth margins, grow at the ends of the branches. These branches are seldom more than 1 m tall and are sparsely covered with reddish-brown glandular hairs. With the approach of autumn the leaves turn spectacular shades of bronze, crimson, and orange.

Clasping-leaved Twisted Stalk

Clasping-leaved Twisted Stalk

Few-flowered Anemone

White-flowered Rhododendron

White-veined Wintergreen; Painted Pyrola W

Pyrola picta WINTERGREEN FAMILY

This unmistakable but rare plant may be identified by its uniquely mottled leaves. The thick, glossy green leaves are strikingly marked on the upper surface with white streaks near the main veins. These pale areas, caused by a lack of chlorophyll, indicate the partially parasitic nature of this plant. From 2 to 20 yellowish-green flowers, often blotched with purple, grow on a single stem, from which they tend to hang sideways. The small sepals have a reddish colour. This choice beauty grows under coniferous trees in the southern limits of our area.

Greenish-flowered Wintergreen BJKWY

Pyrola chlorantha [*P. virens*] WINTERGREEN FAMILY

This wintergreen has a few greenish-white flowers rather loosely spaced around the 10 to 20 cm of the stem. These flowers, which are delicately fragrant, are large and nodding and have 5 waxy petals. The clapper-like style is strongly curved; it protrudes with a distinct collar below the stigma. The anthers are yellow-tipped. After the flowers wither, brown, rounded seed capsules develop. Leaves grow only at the base of the plant. They are long-petioled and broadly elliptical with olive green blades, very finely toothed. Like most wintergreens, this plant prefers the deep shade of coniferous forests.

Leather-leaved Saxifrage BJKWY

Leptarrhena pyrolifolia SAXIFRAGE FAMILY

The basal rosette of leathery, dark glossy-green leaves and the bright red-purple seed capsules are the arresting features of this plant, rather than the flowers. The spoon-shaped, evergreen basal leaves are 3 to 6 cm in size with toothed margins. Up to 3 very small leaves clasp the rigid stem, 10 to 40 cm tall. The small white to pink flowers, each with 10 long stamens, form a dense cluster at the top of each reddish-purple stalk. As the flowers fade, attractive seed capsules develop. Leather-leaved Saxifrage is common along stream banks and on moist slopes in alpine and subalpine habitats.

Mist Maiden; Cliff Romanzoffia BKWY

Romanzoffia sitchensis WATERLEAF FAMILY

Often splashed by the water which drips from melting snows, Mist Maiden is one of the alpine glories within the Canadian Rockies. The basal leaves have 5 to 9 lobes, and the petioles are about twice as long as the blades; there are few, if any, stem leaves. The frail stems seem scarcely strong enough to lift the delicate blossoms above the large, kidney-shaped leaves. The white to cream-coloured flowers, each with a vivid golden-yellow eye, add a charming contrast to the rock crevices in which they grow. The 5 petals are funnel-like at the base, with rounded lobes forming about mid-length. The stamens have white anthers and are uneven in length, while the strap-like sepals are purplish-green. Numerous seeds are contained within the 2-valved fruit.

White-veined Wintergreen

Greenish-flowered Wintergreen

Leather-leaved Saxifrage

Mist Maiden

Cow Parsnip

BJKWY

Heracleum lanatum

PARSNIP FAMILY

This very conspicuous perennial plant, up to 2.5 m tall, towers above its herbaceous neighbours. The prominently ribbed, green, rhubarb-like stems arise from a cluster of slender, parsnip-like roots. These stems bear large leaves (up to 30 cm across), which are deeply lobed, sharp-toothed, 3-parted, and crinkly. They are capped by a myriad of cream-white flowers in large umbrella-like clusters. The fruits are flat and marked on the faces by narrow ribs and dark oil tubes, which extend from the top part-way to the base. Both the flowers and fruits have a pungent but not unpleasant aroma. Most parts of the plant are edible; however, positive identification is required because some similar plants are poisonous. Cow Parsnip has been used for several medicinal purposes, including treatment of arthritis, rheumatism, and intestinal pains. The stems and leaves are palatable to deer, elk, and bears, especially after early autumn frosts. Several species of birds dine on the copious seeds, and bears sometimes eat the flowering heads. Cow Parsnip is found in damp meadows, along stream banks, and in poplar woods.

Birchleaf Spiraea; White Meadowsweet

BJKWY

Spiraea betulifolia [*S. lucida*]

ROSE FAMILY

Spiraeas are very showy shrubs found in the wild as well as in home gardens. Birchleaf Spiraea has cinnamon-brown bark on its erect stems, which are from 30 to 90 cm tall. The leaves are shiny green above and paler beneath, egg-shaped, and deeply notched toward the tips. The creamy flowers, occasionally tinged with pink, are only weakly scented. They are gathered in nearly flat-topped clusters about 4 cm across. The flowers soon turn brownish and after fertilization give way to small, dry, pod-like fruits. Birchleaf Spiraea grows in clearings and on rocky slopes in the montane zone.

Wild Heliotrope; Sitka Valerian

BJKWY

Valeriana sitchensis

VALERIAN FAMILY

This herbaceous perennial is 40 to 80 cm tall and has somewhat succulent, squarish stems arising from a foul-smelling, fleshy rootstock. Large opposite leaves are divided into 3 to 7 coarsely toothed lobes, with progressively shorter petioles up the stem. The small but numerous tubular flowers are crowded into a nearly flat-topped cluster at the top of each stem. Buds and young flowers are pale lavender-pink, the flowers later fading to white. The floral tubes are slightly notched into 5 equal lobes, and 3 stamens and an even longer pistil protrude from the mouth of each flower. After the first frost, what was a vaguely unpleasant odour emitted by the flowers becomes overpowering. When mature, the flat, single-seeded fruits are crowned with numerous feathery bristles that carry seeds far afield on the mountain breezes. The rootstocks were used by Indians as food and also as medicine for stomach ailments; the plant was also used in a tobacco mixture. Several animals eat the leaves and stems of Wild Heliotrope and its flowers attract large numbers of insects.

Cow Parsnip

Birchleaf Spiraea

Wild Heliotrope

Wild Licorice — W

Glycyrrhiza lepidota — PEA FAMILY

Wild Licorice is a coarse perennial, 30 to 100 cm tall, arising from a thick rootstock which has a slight licorice flavour. Leaves consist of 11 to 19 pale green leaflets with conspicuous yellow-brown glands on the lower surface. Numerous showy yellowish-white flowers are borne on short stalks in dense racemes. They are followed by reddish-brown fruits, which are densely beset with short hooked prickles and which persist on the stem through the winter. The rootstocks were roasted and eaten by Indians; they used the plant for a number of other purposes including remedies for fever, toothaches, and earaches. This plant occurs throughout the aspen parkland and prairies on moist slopes, coulees, river banks, and slough margins.

Sweet-flowered Androsace; Rock Jasmine — BJW

Androsace chamaejasme — PRIMROSE FAMILY

Androsace is a small perennial, which grows in tufts at intervals along a creeping stem, producing crowded rosettes of very small linear leaves covered with stiff hairs. These miniature rosettes of tiny leaves support a short stem which bears at its summit a compact cluster of dainty, sweet-scented flowers. The flowers are a soft creamy white with a yellow, orange, or pinkish eye at the centre. This midget of a plant prefers open slopes, meadows, ledges, and screes from subalpine to alpine elevations.

Bronze Bells — BJKWY

Stenanthium occidentale — LILY FAMILY

Bronze Bells has grass-like leaves that emerge from an onion-like bulb. The bell-shaped flowers, greenish and flecked with purple, have 6 sharply pointed tips that twist backward, exposing the interior of the blossom. Ten or more flowers hang gracefully from each stem, 30 to 50 cm tall. The fruit is a sharp-pointed, erect pod. Once you have found this curiously charming plant in the moist, shaded woodlands it prefers, stop and enjoy the tangy fragrance of the flowers.

Partridge Foot; Creeping Spiraea — BJKY

Luetkea pectinata — ROSE FAMILY

Extensive mats of this dwarf evergreen shrub are formed as it creeps on strawberry-like runners over the ground. Its leaves are crowded in basal tufts, and continue alternately up the 5 to 15 cm of the stem. The leaves are small, smooth, and deeply cleft into two, 3-parted sections. Small white (occasionally cream) flowers, with 4 to 6 pistils and about 20 stamens, cluster at the tips of erect stems. Some velvety-green mats, which may be more than a metre across, produce hundreds of such stems. Partridge Foot is generally a rare plant on the east side of the Continental Divide, but it is common in moist, shady areas around timberline in parts of British Columbia.

Wild Licorice

Sweet-flowered Androsace

Bronze Bells

Partridge Foot

Bunchberry; Dwarf Dogwood

BJKWY

Cornus canadensis

DOGWOOD FAMILY

The 4 white "petals" of the Bunchberry are actually bracts surrounding a central cluster of inconspicuous greenish flowers. Later the bracts fade to a brownish colour and the flowers develop into clusters of bland-tasting, cardinal-red berries which are eaten by grouse and other birds. The plant is 8 to 20 cm in height, with a whorl of 4 to 6 dark green leaves, whose tips are sharply pointed. In autumn the leaves turn to brilliant shades of red and purple. The leaves may be used for smoking. Bunchberry grows as individual plants or in dense colonies among the mosses and fallen needles of spruce and pine forests throughout much of Canada.

Wild Strawberry

BJKWY

Fragaria virginiana

ROSE FAMILY

The snowy white petals of the Wild Strawberry contrast with their yellow centres and are accentuated by the plant's many-toothed, green leaflets. The Wild Strawberry is not unlike its cultivated cousin except that the flowers and fruits are generally smaller, and its fruit has an even more delectable flavour than the cultivated variety. Wild Strawberry fruits are eaten by a number of birds and mammals, which disseminate the seeds in their droppings. Wild Strawberry is common from the montane to the alpine region, but while it blooms profusely in the subalpine and alpine region, it frequently does not set fruit because of the cold nights and short growing season. Fresh or dried leaves from this plant can be used to prepare a tea which, being rich in vitamin C, is reported to prevent colds.

Bunchberry

Bunchberry

Wild Strawberry

Wild Strawberry

Yellow Flowers

Yellow Rattle

BJWY

Rhinanthus crista-galli [*R. minor*]

FIGWORT FAMILY

Yellow Rattle is partially parasitic on the roots of other plants, from which it extracts ready-made food. This practice sometimes visibly depresses the growth of grasses and other surrounding plants. The 50-cm-tall flowering stems are erect and may be single or sparsely branched. The leaves are lance-shaped with toothed margins; they grow in opposite pairs, becoming smaller toward the top of the stem. The curious flowers, on a one-sided spike, have yellowish-green calyx tubes which are inflated but flattened along 2 sides and fringed with 4 short teeth. Golden yellow petals form a 2-lipped corolla; the upper lip is 2-lobed and hooded and the lower is 3-lobed. When ripe, the loose seeds in the swollen pods rattle as the wind blows the withering stems—hence the common name. Look for this unusual annual plant in grassy meadows and open woodlands.

Yellow Beardtongue; Yellow Penstemon

BJKWY

Penstemon confertus

FIGWORT FAMILY

The numerous tiny tubular flowers of this delightful species are closely set in several compact whorls along the upper part of the slender stem, the top ring being largest. These rings of sulphur-yellow flowers contrast sharply with the paired green leaves below. Each flower has a tuft of long yellow hairs in its throat, which accounts for the common name. Yellow Beardtongue graces open slopes from low elevations to above timberline.

Silverberry; Wolf Willow

BJKWY

Elaeagnus commutata

OLEASTER FAMILY

This shrub might have been designed by a silversmith, for each leaf, tiny flower, fruit, and new stem or twig is covered with the same rich coating of silvery scales. The rusty-brown branches, from 1 to 3 m tall, are hung with oblong, silvery leaves, from 3 to 8 cm long, which are waxy and smooth-margined. Both surfaces of the leaves have the same striking silver colour, sometimes with scattered brown scales beneath. Each small tubular flower is silvery on the outside and yellowish on the inside, with a strong, sweet scent. The fruits are dry and mealy and contain a single hard seed with 8 striped grooves. Like a tail, the remains of the flower hang onto the end of the silvery fruit. The fruits, too dry and mealy for normal consumption, were resorted to by Indians as a famine food; necklaces were made from the dry seeds. Silverberry is a distinctive shrub of deep coulees, stream banks, and hillsides.

Yellow Rattle

Yellow Beardtongue

Silverberry

Silverberry

Fringed Pinesap WY

Monotropa hypopitys [*Hypopitys monotropa*] INDIAN PIPE FAMILY

There is no chlorophyll in Fringed Pinesap, so its root system is parasitic on saprophytic fungi in the forest humus as a source of nourishment. The entire plant is straw-coloured, occasionally pink to reddish. Its unbranched fleshy stems have leaves that have been reduced to small scales. Each nodding, urn-shaped flower has 4 or 5 petals and 4 or 5 sepals; the terminal flower is the largest, with 5 petals, while the lower ones are smaller, generally with 4 petals. The broad stigma protrudes beyond the petals and the stamens are usually double the number of petals. As the flowers mature they change from a hanging to an erect position. This unique and curious plant is rare. Search for it in deeply shaded pine woods.

Twining Honeysuckle BJKWY

Lonicera dioica HONEYSUCKLE FAMILY

One of the few flowering vines in the Canadian Rocky Mountains, Twining Honeysuckle clambers over low shrubs and around the trunks of trees at low elevations. The trumpet-like flowers cluster in a shallow protective cup formed by 2 leaves that are joined at their bases. The upper leaf surface is bright green and smooth; the underneath is blue-green and downy. When the flowers first open they are yellow, changing to orange-red with age. The 5 petals are united into a funnel-shaped corolla tube, which has a swollen knob near the base where nectar accumulates. Insects puncture the knobs to gain the reserve of sweets. On a calm day the sweet-scented flowers release a drifting trail of heavenly perfume. Red berries eventually replace the flowers within the cupped leaves.

Yellow Columbine BJKWY

Aquilegia flavescens BUTTERCUP FAMILY

Lemon-yellow in colour, occasionally with a dash of pink, the beautiful flowers of the Yellow Columbine nod at the ends of slender stems that lift them above the gracefully divided leaves. Each flower consists of 5 wing-shaped, petal-like sepals; 5 tube-shaped petals, each flaring at the open end and tapering to a distinctive projecting spur at the opposite end; 5 pistils; and numerous stamens. The leaves, which grow from the base of the plant, are compound, long-stalked, and divided into many small segments. The seeds are borne in a 5-parted pod which points upward at maturity. Boiled roots of this plant were used as a cure for diarrhea. Yellow Columbine may be locally common on rocky ledges and screes in the alpine zone, as well as in subalpine glades and along trail verges.

Fringed Pinesap

Twining Honeysuckle

Yellow Columbine

Rough-leaved Alumroot

BJKWY

Heuchera cylindrica

SAXIFRAGE FAMILY

This is a robust plant, at home on rocky slopes and ledges and dry meadows. The leathery leaves, slightly longer than broad, with lobed and toothed margins, are at the base of the plant. Some of the leaves turn bronze or deep red by early autumn. Leafless, wiry stems, 20 to 50 cm high, arise from a thick, scaly rootstock to support the bell-shaped flowers, which are cream to greenish-yellow. An ample store of nectar lures a myriad of insects to the undistinguished flower. Indians were reported to use a decoction of the root as a remedy for diarrhea and as an astringent for sores on horses.

Yellow Heather; Yellow Mountain Heather

BJKWY

Phyllodoce glanduliflora [*P. aleutica*]

HEATH FAMILY

This dwarf evergreen shrub, 10 to 30 cm tall, often shares its habitat with Red Heather. Yellow Heather has yellowish-green, bell-like flowers that are puckered at the open end. The flowers, flower stems, and young branchlets are covered with small sticky hairs; hence the species name *glanduliflora* (glandular flowers). Clusters of nodding flowers are produced on long stalks at the end of the stem. The small, round seed capsules are reddish-coloured. There are grooves on the undersides of the needle-like leaves. Red and Yellow heathers hybridize, and all degrees of variation may be found between the bell-shaped, rose cups of one parent and the vase-shaped, yellowish to greenish-white flowers of the other. Watch for the many-flowered clusters near timberline and in alpine meadows during July and August.

Late Yellow Locoweed

BJKWY

Oxytropis campestris [*O. monticola*]

PEA FAMILY

A highly variable species, Late Yellow Locoweed has flowers that are usually yellowish-white, but white, blue, pink, and purple ones are not too uncommon. Many flowers are borne on stems up to 30 cm high. Each leaf consists of 11 to 31 leaflets with silky hairs on both surfaces. Both the stems and leaves branch from a stout, multiple base. Black and white hairs cover the 4-cm-long seed pods. Domestic livestock that eat these plants appear to suffer mental disorders, hence the name "locoweed." A yellow dye may be produced from both the leaves and the blossoms. Late Yellow Locoweed is common on prairies and in open woodlands.

Rough-leaved Alumroot

Yellow Heather

Late Yellow Locoweed

Bracted Honeysuckle; Black Twinberry — BJKWY

Lonicera involucrata — HONEYSUCKLE FAMILY

Bracted Honeysuckle is a bushy shrub 1 to 2 m tall. Its leaves are between 5 and 15 cm long, elliptical to lance-shaped, veined, and bright green. The shrub is easy to recognize because the flowers, berries, and bracts are paired. The 2 dull yellow flowers, like little twin candles, are cupped by 2 green bracts. The 5 petals of each flower are fused into a funnel-shaped corolla tube; there are no sepals. As the flowers develop into shiny, inky-black berries, the bracts become deep maroon collars which expand backward, exposing more of the twin berries. Although tasting disagreeable to people, the berries are eaten by birds and mammals. This sturdy shrub prefers rather damp, protected places within woodlands.

Goatsbeard — BJKWY

Tragopogon dubius — COMPOSITE FAMILY

Like a giant dandelion, this introduced biennial is a weed of roadsides and other disturbed places. The stout, stiffly erect plant, growing from a deep fleshy taproot, has bluish-green stems and grass-like leaves. When broken, Goatsbeard leaves and stems exude a milky white latex. The pale lemon-yellow ray flowers appear at the end of the stem, which is decidedly thickened below the flower head. There are 10 to 14 pointed involucral bracts, longer than the ray flowers. Perhaps more spectacular than the flower are the achenes with parachute-like attachments that form a globular ball. These are easily broken apart by the wind and the achenes are carried great distances.

Bracted Honeysuckle

Bracted Honeysuckle

Goatsbeard

Goatsbeard

Canadian Buffaloberry; Soapberry — BJKWY

Shepherdia canadensis — OLEASTER FAMILY

This common shrub, 1.5 to 2.5 m tall, grows in several habitats and is often the dominant species in the understory of lodgepole pine woods. Male and female flowers, borne in clusters on separate shrubs, appear on the brown scurfy twigs even before the leaves. The tiny yellowish flowers are inconspicuous; male flowers have 4 stamens while female flowers have none. In the fall, the female shrubs will be covered with small, translucent berries which range in colour from shining yellow to red. The thick, leathery leaves are green and glossy on the upper surface, while the lower surface is covered with a white felt and sprinkled with rusty dots. All parts of the plant are covered with rust-coloured, shiny scales. Although repulsive to us, the berries are enjoyed by birds and mammals, being particularly important to grizzly and black bears. Whipped with a little water, the berries produce a pink, foamy drink that was much prized by many Indians. Crush a berry between your fingers and note the soapy feel that results from the presence of the glucoside saponin, which is now used as a foaming agent in detergents.

Oregon Grape; Creeping Mahonia — BKWY

Berberis repens [*Mahonia repens*] — BARBERRY FAMILY

Oregon Grape is a creeping shrub, generally from 10 to 30 cm tall. Its holly-like leaves are waxy and leathery with prickly margins. Each leaf consists of 3 to 7 dark, glossy green leaflets. With the arrival of autumn, some of the leaves change to a flaming glory of red and purple. The handsome foliage is a suitable background for clusters of rich golden-yellow flowers. Each flower has 6 petals, 6 sepals, and 6 stamens. After the flowers' work is done, they are replaced by juicy blue berries that gleam amid the leaves. Indians ate the berries, extracted yellow dyes from the roots, and used the bark of roots as a medicine and tonic. This plant is at home on rocky slopes and in open forests.

Canadian Buffaloberry

Canadian Buffaloberry

Oregon Grape

Puccoon; Stoneseed

BKW

Lithospermum ruderale

BORAGE FAMILY

This is a coarse perennial, up to 50 cm high, that is firmly anchored to dry slopes and grasslands by a large woody taproot. Numerous sharply pointed, lance-shaped leaves clasp the stem. The small flowers are not particularly showy, being lemon-yellow or greenish and partly hidden in the axils of the leaves near the top of the stem, but they have a strong and pleasing scent. Both the stems and leaves are covered with long white hairs. *Lithospermum* means "stoneseed," which is an apt description of the plant's extremely hard nutlets. For centuries some Indians used an extract of this plant for birth control. Natural estrogens in the plant suppress the release of certain hormones required for ovulation. The roots were used as food and as a source of red dye.

Common Mullein

WY

Verbascum thapsus

FIGWORT FAMILY

This Eurasian import grows to about 1 or 2 m tall. It is a biennial. From the first-year rosette of large velvet-like leaves surges the strong sentinel-like stalk during the second year. Over a period of many days, pleasant-smelling yellow flowers open up and down the flowering spike in no apparent order. The 3 upper stamens have densely hairy filaments while the 2 lower ones are smooth; all 5 have showy orange anthers. The pistil is prominent and club-topped. After flowering, the dead stem, changing to a dark brown colour, may persist for many months. Common Mullein grows along roadsides and in other disturbed areas within the montane zone.

Butter-and-Eggs; Yellow Toadflax

BWY

Linaria vulgaris

FIGWORT FAMILY

Despite its reputation as a noxious weed, this Eurasian introduction is a striking plant. From 20 to 80 cm tall, the upright stems of this perennial grow from creeping roots. The grey-green leaves are alternate, narrow, and stalkless. Butter-and-Eggs has snapdragon-like flowers 2 or 3 cm long, each with a long, tapered spur. The tube and corolla are lemon-yellow with a brilliant orange pouch on the lower lip. This plant is found along roadsides and other disturbed areas.

Flame-coloured Lousewort

BJ

Pedicularis flammea

FIGWORT FAMILY

Of the several louseworts that grow in our area, this is one of the most attractive. The upright, reddish-purple stem is about 10 cm high. It bears a spike of fascinating flowers which look like miniature parrot bills. True to the name *flammea*, the colour is indeed flame-like, with the lower lip yellow and the upper one purple to deep-crimson. The leaves are pinnately divided and lacy. Although the Flame-coloured Lousewort is rare, it is immediately noticeable because of its brilliant flowers. Search for it on calcareous alpine slopes.

Puccoon

Common Mullein

Butter-and-Eggs

Flame-coloured Lousewort

Yellow Dryad

BJKWY

Dryas drummondii

ROSE FAMILY

This handsome species is distinguished by its pale to bright yellow nodding flowers, on slender stems 15 to 25 cm tall. There are 8 to 10 petals, which never open fully. The sepals are densely covered with a dark, bumpy coat of hairs. Silken plumes later replace the flowers as the styles become twisted into a shiny top. The tiny seeds await a wind to float them away on parachute-like styles to populate new habitats. The wrinkled, leathery evergreen leaves are dark green above, contrasting with the white, hairy lower surface. This plant has a tough woody stem from which slender branches spread above the ground to form mats of leafy stems. It is a common pioneer on gravel flats, rocky slopes, and roadsides in the montane zone, where the lack of competition allows it to form extensive carpets up to 2 m in diameter.

Sibbaldia

BJKWY

Sibbaldia procumbens

ROSE FAMILY

A rather common but inconspicuous plant, this wee herbaceous perennial prefers stable alpine slopes. Branching from a woody base, the stems terminate in clusters of 3-parted, wedge-shaped leaflets, each with 3 prominent teeth at the blunt end and white hairs on both surfaces. The leaves resemble miniature strawberry leaves. Heads are few-flowered and consist of 5 small, pale yellow petals, like dabs of butter, alternating with larger dark green sepals. There are only 5 stamens, an unusual feature among the Rose Family. Instead of producing juicy berries, Sibbaldia develops small achenes on a dry receptacle.

Mountain Meadow Cinquefoil

BJKWY

Potentilla diversifolia

ROSE FAMILY

Mountain Meadow Cinquefoil is a common and highly variable plant that grows from the subalpine to high exposed rocky ridges. Its leaves are nearly all basal, each having 5 to 7 leaflets with forward-pointing teeth along the upper two-thirds of their margins. The slender flowering stalks are often reddish, and grow from 10 to 40 cm in height. Generally, 3 to 5 bright yellow flowers are well spaced near the stem tip. The plant may be either hairy or smooth. Depending on the elevation, the flowering period runs from June into August.

Yellow Dryad

Yellow Dryad

Sibbaldia

Mountain Meadow Cinquefoil

Alpine Cinquefoil

BJKWY

Potentilla nivea

ROSE FAMILY

Alpine Cinquefoil is a dwarf perennial with a stout stem-base and numerous small, 3-parted leaves that hug the ground in a dense cushion or mat. These silvery-green leaves are densely clothed with coarse greyish hairs, somewhat less dense on the top than underneath. The hairs reduce the intensity of the sunlight and protect the stomata from the full force of the winds, thus preventing excessive water loss. The stems, 10 to 20 cm tall, scarcely lift the golden-yellow flowers above the cluster of leaves. *Potentilla* is a large and notoriously difficult group to identify, with about 30 species in our area. Recognition of the genus is easy, however, as there is an extra set of 5 bracts below the 5 petals and 5 sepals. This silvery little cinquefoil, with its vivid splashes of golden blossoms, adds colour to rocky and exposed slopes in the high alpine region.

Lyall's Iron Plant

BJKY

Haplopappus lyallii

COMPOSITE FAMILY

This sturdy mountain-dweller will be found only by those wayfarers with strong legs and keen eyes. It is a dwarf perennial, generally less than 10 cm high. The small lance-shaped leaves, 2 to 6 cm long, are hairy and often covered with a sticky coating. The leaves are clumped mainly at the base of the flower stem. The solitary flower head is a deep yellow and appears incongruously large compared to the rest of the tiny plant. Both the ray and disk flowers are yellow, while the involucral bracts are purple-tipped and sticky. Lyall's Iron Plant forms small clumps on shaly slopes above treeline and is easily confused with Golden Fleabane, which is much more common. Lyall's Iron Plant, however, has sessile leaves in contrast to petiolate leaves on the latter.

Balsamroot

KW

Balsamorhiza sagittata

COMPOSITE FAMILY

This striking plant is limited in distribution to open sunny areas in the southern portion of the Canadian Rockies. Balsamroot, so named because it grows from a strong-smelling taproot, has clumps of arrowhead-shaped basal leaves up to 30 cm long and 15 cm wide. They are silver-grey in colour, with a dense cover of woolly, white hairs on both sides. Bright yellow, sunflower-like blossoms, up to 10 cm across, are borne singly at the end of long stalks. Although generally shunned by domestic livestock, Balsamroot is grazed by deer, elk, and mountain sheep. Indians used to eat the stout starchy roots and tender young shoots. This plant blooms in May, spreading a carpet of yellow across the grassy slopes of the southern mountains and foothills.

Alpine Cinquefoil

Lyall's Iron Plant

Balsamroot

Brown-eyed Susan; Wild Gaillardia — BJKWY

Gaillardia aristata — COMPOSITE FAMILY

Across a grassland on a hot day in July or early August, there is nothing like a troop of showy Brown-eyed Susans to gladden the heart, for the big brown eyes seem to wink a friendly greeting as they sway in the breeze. The terminal flower heads, up to 8 cm across, consist of disk and ray flowers. Purplish-brown central disk flowers are surrounded by striking golden ray flowers whose individual "petals" have 3-cleft tips. The lower leaves are lance-shaped and the others, on a stem 30 to 80 cm tall, are toothed. An abundance of greyish-green hairs covers the entire plant. Brown-eyed Susans are found on dry grasslands at low elevations.

Slender Hawkweed; Alpine Hawkweed — BJKWY

Hieracium gracile — COMPOSITE FAMILY

Slender Hawkweed is a herb growing 10 to 30 cm tall in subalpine and alpine meadows and on rocky slopes in open coniferous woods. The basal leaves have long petioles and sparingly toothed margins. They vary from lance- to spatula-shaped. The erect flowering stem may have one or more leaves, but they are small and lack petioles. Three or more small heads with pale yellow ray flowers are produced on the stem. A black, woolly collar surrounds each flower head and protects the tender buds from penetrating frost and drying winds. As well, the stem and branches of the flowering part of the plant are covered with dense, grey down and long, black hairs. When ripe the fruit is chestnut-brown with white bristles.

Hairy Golden Aster — BKWY

Chrysopsis villosa [*Heterotheca villosa*] — COMPOSITE FAMILY

This much-branched perennial, growing from a woody taproot, may be erect, but it is more often sprawling. The upper grey-green leaves are entire, and narrowly to broadly lance-shaped; they grow alternately along the stem. The lower leaves wither early. All green parts of the plant are covered with soft white hairs. Rich golden-yellow, multi-petalled ray flowers and orange to brown tubular disk flowers form heads at the end of each branch. Involucral bracts are overlapping, pointed, fuzzy, and slender. Hairy Golden Aster prefers dry sandy soil with full exposure to the sun.

Brown-eyed Susan

Slender Hawkweed

Hairy Golden Aster

Alpine Poppy

BJ

Papaver kluanensis

POPPY FAMILY

Not unlike the poppies in our home gardens and parks, the Alpine Poppy has 4 petals that form a cup. The petals enclose a star-shaped stigma, which is ringed by a crown of stamens. All visible parts of the plant, except for the flower, are covered with hairs. Hairs on the leaf blades and petioles are white while those on the oval bud are dark brown. The numerous 5-lobed leaves are all basal. As the sulphur-yellow petals grow older they often become pale green. The flat-topped ovary later develops into the familiar seed capsule, ringed with small openings at the top which allow the wind to scatter the many seeds. Alpine Poppy is by no means common even in its favourite habitat among the rocks and ledges at high altitudes.

Golden Bean; Buffalo Bean

BKWY

Thermopsis rhombifolia

PEA FAMILY

Closely resembling a yellow-flowered lupine, Golden Bean is one of the most striking and colourful early spring flowers. Stout, branched stems of this perennial usually grow in large patches from running rootstocks. The 10- to 40-cm stems have alternate leaves, each with 3 egg-shaped leaflets 2 or 3 cm long. Bright golden-yellow flowers cluster in a showy raceme from 5 to 12 cm long. The pea-like flowers are succeeded by greyish-brown, hairy pods, which are often curved in a semicircle and whose fruits are poisonous. One common name, Buffalo Bean, was applied to the plant by Indians because they used its flowering season as an indicator that buffalo bulls were in prime condition for spring hunting. Flowering in May and early June, the plant is common in dry, sandy grasslands.

Yellow Monkey Flower

BW

Mimulus guttatus

FIGWORT FAMILY

Yellow Monkey Flower varies a great deal, but it is always spectacular. It may be an annual or a perennial, a ground-hugging dwarf or a robust plant 100 cm high; the stems may be erect or trailing; the leaves may be smooth or covered with soft hairs; and the lower flower lip may have a single large crimson spot or many smaller spots. These flowers are like snapdragons, 2 to 4 cm long, bright yellow, trumpet-shaped, with crimson to brownish-red dots on the larger lower lip. Also, the corolla tube is delicately haired and distinctly 2-lipped, with prominent ridges in the throat. The stem is succulent, hollow, and squarish, and the leaves are well spaced along it, growing in pairs on opposite sides of the stem. After the corolla has fallen, the whole calyx inflates until in fruit it is large and conspicuous. Sunny moist areas, such as springs and mossy banks of mountain streams, are favoured habitats and this plant may dominate such areas with bright patches of shimmering golden blooms.

Alpine Poppy

Golden Bean

Yellow Monkey Flower

Sandberg's Wild Parsley — W

Lomatium sandbergii — PARSNIP FAMILY

A dwarf alpine plant of screes, Sandberg's Wild Parsley grows close to the ground, except for the flower stalks, which may elongate up to 20 cm. The bright green leaves have petioles and the blades are finely divided like those of parsley. The main umbel, with bright yellow flowers, may be 4 cm wide; there are smaller secondary umbels. Individual flowers are tiny, but numerous within a compound umbel. Oblong fruits with narrow marginal wings soon replace the flowers.

Meadow Parsnip; Heart-leaved Alexanders — BJWY

Zizia aptera — PARSNIP FAMILY

Meadow Parsnip has yellow flower clusters that are held above their leaves like dainty umbrellas. The leaves are variable in shape and size. Basal leaves are long-petioled and heart-shaped; stem leaves are smaller, short-petioled, and divided into 3 leaflets. Stem leaves become progressively smaller along the stem until they become cleft leaflets. The somewhat flattened fruits are ribbed and greenish-brown in colour. This member of the carrot family is most likely to be found in damp meadows up to timberline.

Yellowbell; Yellow Fritillary — W

Fritillaria pudica — LILY FAMILY

Restricted in distribution to the southern part of our area, the strikingly beautiful flowers of Yellowbell herald the arrival of spring. It grows from a small, scaly, white bulb about 1 cm across. The bulbs, 5 to 30 cm beneath the ground surface, reproduce asexually by forming grain-sized offsets. The stems stand 10 to 30 cm tall and carry from 2 to 6 blue-green, strap-shaped leaves about 8 cm long. The flowers are narrowly bell-shaped with similar petals and sepals about 2 cm long; they hang demurely like solitary bells from the end of their curved stems. The chromatic yellow flowers, etched faintly with fine purple lines, turn orange to brick-red on aging. After the petals and sepals fall off, the stems straighten out and place the stout, 3-parted fruits in an erect position. The bulbs and offsets were used as food by the Indians and early explorers and are eagerly sought by small mammals. This charming plant inhabits sheltered grasslands and coulees at low elevations.

Sandberg's Wild Parsley

Meadow Parsnip

Yellowbell

Double Bladder Pod BJKWY

Physaria didymocarpa MUSTARD FAMILY

Growing on fully exposed, dry, stony ground where there is little competition from other plants, Double Bladder Pod is anchored by a deep taproot. The cluster of fan-shaped basal leaves is mealy-white. Each leaf blade is blunt and shallowly notched, and densely covered with silvery hairs. The weak stems, often trailing on the ground, have much smaller leaves and support a short terminal cluster of cross-shaped, bright yellow flowers. Pairs of swollen seed pods, purplish-green in colour, give the plant a distinctive character as they mature. Juice from the plant is reported to have been used by Indians for sore throats, cramps, and stomach trouble.

Yellow Draba; Yellow Whitlow Grass BJKWY

Draba paysonii MUSTARD FAMILY

Several drabas with pale to bright yellow flowers grow in the alpine region. They are low-growing, tufted plants with small cross-shaped flowers consisting of 4 sepals, 4 petals, 6 stamens, and 1 pistil. Discrimination between the various species is often difficult, but several of the high-elevation species are enchantingly lovely. This particular species is a matted plant scarcely 10 or 12 cm tall. It has numerous leaves, with branched hairs, and clusters of tiny yellow flowers at the ends of the stems. The flowers may be used to make dyes of cream, gold, and chartreuse.

Evergreen Violet; Round-leaved Violet BJKWY

Viola orbiculata VIOLET FAMILY

This dwarf species has bright yellow flowers streaked with violet. The violet lines converge on the lower petals and guide insects to the nectar-secreting glands, which are enclosed within the spur. Both the basal leaves and flower stalks rise from a scaly rootstock. The roundish leaves are smooth with toothed margins, and they generally remain green through the winter. Candied flowers of this plant can be used for decorating cakes and pastries. Evergreen Violet inhabits moist woods in the montane zone, especially sites with damp moss. It blooms early in the season.

Double Bladder Pod

Yellow Draba

Evergreen Violet

Glacier Lily; Dog-toothed Violet BJKWY

Erythronium grandiflorum LILY FAMILY

Standing out like splashes of gold against the white edges of melting snowdrifts, these flowers are one of the first harbingers of spring, impatient to brighten the slopes as the snowbanks retreat. The nodding yellow flowers are on stems 15 to 30 cm high. The 6 taper-pointed "petals" (actually 3 petals and 3 sepals) curl back, exposing 6 yellow stamens and the style to full view. Two large, broad, pointed leaves grow from the base of the plant; they are a shiny light green. After the petals and sepals fall, an erect, many-seeded capsule develops. The small, deep-set corms are eagerly eaten by both black and grizzly bears. Dense patches of Glacier Lily can be found in open timberline forests and alpine meadows.

Creeping Buttercup; Seaside Buttercup BJKWY

Ranunculus cymbalaria BUTTERCUP FAMILY

This buttercup spreads over the ground by slender creeping stems or trailing runners, much like those of strawberries. The long-petioled leaf blades are egg- to heart-shaped, with scalloped margins. These characteristic leaves distinguish it from other buttercups with the same creeping habit. The flowering stems are leafless and have one to several small yellow flowers. Several small achenes, with short straight beaks and prominent longitudinal ribs, form a cylindrical seed head. Creeping Buttercup is a plant of muddy shores and brackish ponds.

Alpine Buttercup; Snow Buttercup BJKWY

Ranunculus eschscholtzii BUTTERCUP FAMILY

This dainty but hardy dwarf buttercup will be seen only by those who venture near or above timberline. Five bright yellow petals, 5 lavender-tinged sepals, and numerous stamens and pistils form the flower. The flower, about 2.5 cm across and appearing too large for such a small plant, emerges in the spring or early summer before the stems have reached their full length. As the seed cluster matures, the plant may reach 25 or 30 cm in height. The leaves are mainly basal, each 3- to 5-parted, and deeply toothed. Alpine Buttercup often grows in pools of water from melting snow, along streams and ponds, and in meadows.

Dwarf Buttercup BJKY

Ranunculus pygmaeus BUTTERCUP FAMILY

A tiny perennial plant, Dwarf Buttercup bears one to several single-flowered stems above its basal leaves. The leaves are deeply divided into 3 main lobes, with each lobe split again. The 5 yellow petals and 5 greenish sepals are about the same length. A head of short-beaked achenes soon replaces the flowers. This tiny plant may be found on moist alpine slopes and rocky ledges.

Glacier Lily

Creeping Buttercup

Alpine Buttercup

Dwarf Buttercup

Spider Plant BJ

Saxifraga flagellaris SAXIFRAGE FAMILY

Spider Plant is a true alpine dweller and, at the southern limit of its range, is one of the rarest plants within our area. A distinctive feature of this plant is its radiating whip-like, arching runners, each terminating in a tiny rooting offset, not unlike a strawberry plant. The spider-like appearance of the runners gave rise to the common name. A solitary stem arises from compact basal rosettes of leaves; it is leafy and covered with glandular bumps. The basal leaves are 5 to 10 mm long with bristle-like white hairs on the margins. The solitary stem generally produces 1 to 3 brilliant, golden-yellow flowers, often with pink spots near the inner base. Our Rocky Mountains contain a few of these jewels, which are highly valued by the wildflower enthusiast since they are difficult to find. Look for Spider Plant on limestone areas on moist, turfy alpine slopes and ridges.

Yellow Mountain Saxifrage BJKY

Saxifraga aizoides SAXIFRAGE FAMILY

Loose mats or cushions of this sturdy little plant, standing out like splashes of yellow gold when in bloom, are found on moist sand, gravel, and stony débris to well above timberline. The upright stems are 5 to 10 cm tall and crowded with fat, succulent leaves, linear in shape with an abrupt tip. Small clumps of stems are topped by a few pale yellow flowers often spotted with orange. The 5 long and narrow petals are slightly ragged at their tips. The 10 stamens have conspicuously large anthers and there is generally a pair of plump carpels. Depending on the species and the part of the plant used, saxifrages yield yellow-gold to greenish-yellow dyes.

Shrubby Cinquefoil BJKWY

Potentilla fruticosa ROSE FAMILY

As the common name suggests, this plant is a flowering shrub. The woody stems may be either spreading or erect and from 30 to 125 cm in height. The brown bark of the stem peels off in long strips. The greyish-green leaves consist of 3 to 7 closely crowded leaflets, which are lightly hairy, often curled, with smooth margins. Golden-yellow, buttercup-like flowers bloom from June through September, one of the longest blooming periods of any plant within our area. Flowers tend to be small and pale at low elevations and much larger and brighter at high altitudes. Shrubby Cinquefoil is found over a wide variety of habitats ranging from prairies to alpine slopes. Because of their great beauty, domesticated varieties are frequently grown in gardens as ornamental shrubs. When growing in abundance, such as near the eastern boundary of Waterton Lakes National Park, its presence indicates overgrazing by domestic livestock.

Spider Plant

Yellow Mountain Saxifrage

Shrubby Cinquefoil

Fringed Loosestrife W

Lysimachia ciliata PRIMROSE FAMILY

Fringed Loosestrife is an erect plant 30 to 100 cm high. Its green, opposite leaves are pointed at the end and rounded at the base. Both the leaf margins and the petioles are fringed with white hairs. Borne in the upper leaf axils, the large flowers have 5 bright yellow petals with somewhat unevenly pointed tips and reddish glandular bases. The 5 fertile stamens alternate with 5 sterile stamens. This plant prefers moist or boggy places in the montane zone.

Dwarf Mountain Groundsel BJKWY

Senecio fremontii COMPOSITE FAMILY

Often growing in loose sprawling clumps on scree slopes of the alpine or subalpine zones, Dwarf Mountain Groundsel is a distinctive member of the genus *Senecio*. The leaves are somewhat fleshy, lance- to wedge-shaped, and have rather coarse, shallowly toothed margins. They occur alternately along the simple or sparsely branched stems. Relatively large, often wine-red, solitary heads form at the top of stems. Only a few bright yellow ray flowers are present in each head.

Common Stonecrop BJKWY

Sedum lanceolatum STONECROP FAMILY

Like all species of *Sedum*, the Common Stonecrop grows in clumps and has fleshy stems and leaves. The numerous basal leaves, almost round in cross-section, form a rosette. The petals are bright yellow, with sharp points, and they are distinctly separate right to the base. They form a compact cluster at the top of a stem that is 10 to 15 cm high. The long golden stamens are conspicuous. Both the succulent leaves and stems store water to ensure the plant's survival during drought. The young stems and leaves are reported to be good eating when cooked. Common Stonecrop grows on screes and thin gravelly soils from lower elevations to well above timberline.

Fringed Loosestrife

Dwarf Mountain Groundsel

Common Stonecrop

Yellow-flowered False Dandelion BJKW

Agoseris glauca COMPOSITE FAMILY

The vivid yellow heads of this False Dandelion are usually passed over as just another dandelion, but upon closer examination several differences are apparent. False Dandelion leaves are narrower and much longer, while the leaf blades are smooth or faintly toothed rather than deeply incised. In addition, the bracts of the heads are broader and never turned back along the stem as they are in the introduced dandelion. The plant shares many characteristics with the dandelions, including a long taproot, a rosette of basal leaves, a single yellow flower head borne on a long stalk, and a sticky milky juice. Both the leaves and stems are usually blue-green with white hairs, or they may be nearly hairless. The flower heads, 2 to 5 cm across, are yellow when young, but often turn pinkish at maturity. Yellow-flowered False Dandelion is a common species that is widely distributed in open habitats from the montane to the alpine zone.

Orange-flowered False Dandelion; Orange Agoseris BJKWY

Agoseris aurantiaca COMPOSITE FAMILY

This perennial plant, 10 to 50 cm tall, looks like a dandelion with reddish-orange flowers. Two or more rosettes of long, slender leaves with smooth or slightly toothed margins are produced from a woody taproot. The leafless stem is smooth except for white and woolly hairs under a solitary flower head. When fresh, the flowers are a burnt orange colour, drying to deep pink or purple. Their outer floral bracts are narrow, often spotted with purple along the midrib. Tufts of long white hairs, like silken shuttlecocks, are attached to the end of each seed and ensure that they are scattered by the wind. A milky juice exudes from the stems and leaves when broken. Like the Common Dandelion, this plant can be used for salads, potherbs, tea, and wine. Orange-flowered False Dandelion grows on open slopes and meadows to slightly above timberline.

Northern Dandelion BJKWY

Taraxacum ceratophorum COMPOSITE FAMILY

Most of the dandelions seen in our national parks are the introduced Common Dandelion, *Taraxacum officinale*. There are a few native species, such as the Northern Dandelion, which are comparatively rare and usually found high in the mountains. The general characteristics of dandelions are similar: heads of the brightest yellow; ray flowers on hollow stems; deeply toothed, lance-shaped leaves; milky sap in the stems and leaves; and a rounded seed head full of parachute-like seeds that drift far and wide. The leaves and flowering stems rise from a fleshy taproot. All parts of the dandelion may be used for food or drink. The greens are used as salad, potherb, or a tea; the roots roasted for a coffee substitute; and the blossoms fermented for wine. This plant has also been used for a host of medicinal purposes. Bears are particularly fond of the dandelion flowers, as evidenced by their yellow-stained muzzles during the flowering period. Look for Northern Dandelion on open slopes of the alpine region.

Yellow-flowered False Dandelion

Orange-flowered False Dandelion

Northern Dandelion

Yellow Lady's Slipper — BJY

Cypripedium calceolus — ORCHID FAMILY

This is one of the most exquisite of nature's creations. Both scientific names mean "slipper" or "small shoe," referring to the resemblance of the flower's satiny, sun-golden, inflated pouch to a slipper. This bladder-like pouch is lined with purple streaks and spots that add even more to its beauty. The lateral petals may be quite variable in colour, ranging from yellowish- or greenish- to purplish-brown; they are often spirally twisted. The perfumed flowers are supported on stems 30 to 60 cm tall. Large, prominently veined, clasping leaves provide an elegant background for the unique flowers. Yellow Lady's Slipper grows as an individual plant or in crowded clumps in moist forests and mossy bogs. While it is common in some locations, it has disappeared from others because of its susceptibility to being picked.

Nodding Scorzonella — W

Microseris nutans — COMPOSITE FAMILY

With only a casual glance Nodding Scorzonella might be mistaken for a dandelion, but it has very sharply pointed, narrow leaves, pappus bristles, and black hairs on the bracts that grip the flower head. This slender perennial, growing from a fleshy taproot, produces solitary heads on long unbranched, leafless stalks. The flower heads are nodding in bud, becoming erect in blossom. Their outer, pale yellow ray flowers, sometimes veined with purple, are longer than the inner ones. There are no disk flowers. Like dandelions, the seeds are tipped with silvery-white, feathery "parachutes." Found only in the southern part of our area, this plant is fairly common in dry meadows and open woods at middle elevations.

Rocky Mountain Goldenrod — BJKWY

Solidago multiradiata — COMPOSITE FAMILY

Rocky Mountain Goldenrod has a woody rootstock and erect, leafy (often reddish) stems, which bear dense clusters of golden-yellow flower heads. Most often, 8 ray florets surround 13 or more disk florets. The inner bracts of the flower head are much longer than the outer ones, although all are blunt-ended. The leaves, which are nearly spoon-shaped or lance-shaped, with deeply impressed midribs, occur in clumps at the plant's base and also along the stem. Basal leaves have white, hairy-margined petioles, which distinguish this species from Dwarf Goldenrod (*S. spathulata*). Plants may be up to 40 cm tall, but are usually much smaller, around 6 cm, at high elevations. The flowers produce a gold to yellow dye. Certain species of goldenrod are believed to have wound-healing properties. This plant is common on dry, open slopes to above the timberline.

Nodding Scorzonella

Yellow Lady's Slipper

Rocky Mountain Goldenrod

Lake Louise Arnica BJKW

Arnica louiseana COMPOSITE FAMILY

A tiny alpine plant with large, yellow, daisy-like flowers, Lake Louise Arnica is found on open slopes and along brooks at high altitudes. Usually the flower head is borne singly (occasionally in twos or threes) at the top of a short, stout stem. The heads nod or hang in a graceful fashion to within a few centimetres of the ground. The involucral bracts are nearly hairless except near the base. Oblong to broadly lance-shaped leaves, often toothed, are attached at the base of the plant by short petioles. Small stem leaves may also be present.

Alpine Hawksbeard; Dwarf Hawksbeard BJKWY

Crepis nana COMPOSITE FAMILY

Another sturdy dweller of high elevations is Alpine Hawksbeard. This little gem with its bright yellow flower heads, like flecks of gold among the scree and rocks in which it grows, is anchored firmly in the soil by a long taproot. A dwarf perennial, it has bluish-green leaves, with long petioles and spoon-shaped blades, forming a flat rosette tight against the ground. The short flower stems are barely elevated above the leafy rosette. Golden brown fruits with white, downy tails soon replace the tiny yellow blooms. Only the fortunate wayfarer will find this lovely treasure, for it inhabits the high places where few people wander.

Heartleaf Arnica BJKWY

Arnica cordifolia COMPOSITE FAMILY

Heartleaf Arnica is the most common of the 15 species of arnica in the southern Canadian Rockies. Its cheerful lemon-yellow flowers, 5 to 8 cm across, are among the most conspicuous of all mountain flowers, glistening above the heart-shaped lower leaves from which the common name was derived. The leaves have serrated edges. The stems may be between 35 and 70 cm tall, often with one large flower head and two smaller lateral ones. Openings in coniferous woods are the favoured habitat of this daisy-like flower.

Golden Fleabane BJKY

Erigeron aureus COMPOSITE FAMILY

This dwarf perennial plant produces bright golden-yellow flower heads which, like those of several other alpine plants, appear too large for the small size of the plant. The solitary flower heads may span 2 or 3 cm, while the stems are only 2 to 15 cm tall. Bracts on the flower heads are purplish, or at least have a purplish tip, and are covered with woolly hairs. Deep green oval leaves branch on short petioles from the central rootstock in a small rosette. There may also be a few smaller stem leaves. With its 25 to 70 yellow ray florets surrounding yellow disk florets, Golden Fleabane is considered by many flower lovers to be the loveliest of the many fleabanes. Golden Fleabane may be locally common on turfy alpine slopes.

Lake Louise Arnica

Alpine Hawksbeard

Heartleaf Arnica

Golden Fleabane

Black-tipped Groundsel BJKY

Senecio lugens COMPOSITE FAMILY

A distinctive plant, Black-tipped Groundsel is one of the multitude of brilliant wildflowers that bedeck alpine meadows. The large, erect leaves vertically encircle stout stems which culminate in crowns of yellow blooms. At maturity, a wealth of silken-haired seeds supplants the flowers and is spread near and far by the wind. The conspicuous black-tipped bracts are useful in identifying this species. These bracts were considered by the Inuit to be a sign of mourning for a band of unsuspecting Inuit massacred in 1771 by Indian warriors who accompanied the explorer Samuel Hearne on his expedition to the Arctic Coast. Sir John Richardson first collected this plant near the massacre site, Bloody Falls on the Coppermine River, and named it *lugens* (from the Latin word meaning "to mourn").

Prairie Groundsel BJKWY

Senecio canus COMPOSITE FAMILY

Prairie Groundsel is a white woolly perennial, whose horizontal rootstock produces stems up to 40 cm tall. The clustered basal leaves have short petioles and no teeth. Leaves of the flowering stem, although variable, are smaller with toothed margins. In early summer the branching stems carry heads of bright yellow flowers in an open umbel. The involucral bracts are uniformly green. Green parts of the plant, and especially the underside of the leaves, are densely coated with hair. Although this plant is typical of the prairies, it may be found in dry and exposed sites almost to timberline.

Triangular-leaved Ragwort; Giant Ragwort BJKWY

Senecio triangularis COMPOSITE FAMILY

This ragwort is a coarse perennial with several tall, erect, and very leafy stems. The leaves are triangular, with long points, and they are borne singly along the stem, which is 60 to 120 cm tall. Large lower leaves, with jagged margins, have long petioles, but the smaller upper ones have no petioles and their margins have smaller teeth. The stems are smooth and generally purplish at the base, crowned with quite a showy terminal cluster of flowers. The open, flat-topped cluster may have only a few or many flower heads, each with 5 to 12 deep yellow rays. These plants are often found in large clumps or colonies along streams or in meadows of the subalpine region.

Black-tipped Groundsel

Prairie Groundsel

Triangular-leaved Ragwort

Pink, Red & Orange Flowers

Old Man's Whiskers; Three-flowered Avens; Prairie Smoke

BJKWY

Geum triflorum

ROSE FAMILY

Another harbinger of spring, the bright green, fern-like leaves of Old Man's Whiskers surround a stem crowned with three short-stalked flowers. In addition to basal leaves, the flowering stem has a cluster of leaves halfway up and another just below the nodding flowers. Soft hairs cover the whole plant. The purplish-red sepals of the urn-shaped flowers open just wide enough to expose the cream to pinkish petals. Later the 3 nodding flower stalks grow erect as the flowers are replaced by a mist of feathery plumes that soon scatter, like wind-blown parachutes. Old Man's Whiskers is a common perennial from dry grasslands to subalpine meadows. Various parts of the plant were used by Indians as a treatment for swollen eyes, as perfume, and as a tonic.

Nodding Onion

BJKWY

Allium cernuum

LILY FAMILY

The onion-like essence that is released at the least bruising of its tissues proclaims the generic relationship of Nodding Onion. Its pinkish-lavender (rarely white) flower heads, nodding above grass-like leaves, suggest a number of little bells with the long style and stamens protruding beyond the petals. With maturity the nodding stalks rise until the dry capsules stand stiffly erect. The leaves are circular but not hollow. Both the leaves and flower cluster arise from a purple bulb with a black membranous coating. The bulbs and the leaves were eaten raw or used as flavouring by Indians and early settlers. This onion is common in grasslands and meadows from the montane to the alpine.

Twinflower

BJKWY

Linnaea borealis

HONEYSUCKLE FAMILY

Of the thousands of plants known to Linnaeus, the father of modern plant nomenclature, Twinflower was his favourite. This elegant, sweet-scented, trailing evergreen is common in coniferous forests throughout our region, but is easily overlooked. Its runners creep over the forest floor, over moss, rotting logs, and stumps alike. At frequent intervals the runners give rise to Y-shaped stems 5 to 10 cm tall. Each fork of the stem supports at its end a demure, slightly flared, pink, trumpet-like flower, which hangs like a tiny lantern on a miniature lamp-post. Within the trumpet are 2 long and 2 short stamens. The flowers emit an incredibly sweet perfume, which is most evident near evening. The plant's dry fruit has hooked bristles that readily become attached to the fur of mammals or the feathers of birds. The leaves, on opposite sides of the stem, are broadly elliptical with a few blunt teeth above the middle on each side. Kootenay Indians are reported to have made tea from the leaves.

Old Man's Whiskers

Old Man's Whiskers

Nodding Onion

Twinflower

Alpine Milkvetch BJKWY

Astragalus alpinus PEA FAMILY

A low mat-forming herb, Alpine Milkvetch arises from creeping rhizomes that support delicate stems from 10 to 20 cm tall. These stems bear leaves with 13 to 25 leaflets, which are greenish in colour, elliptical in shape, and have white, bristly hairs beneath and appressed hairs above. The flowers, borne in crowded clusters along the ends of the stems, are two-toned in colour with the standard and tip of the keel a pale, bluish-violet and the wings and rest of the corolla white. Sharply pointed at both ends, the pendulous pods are brown and densely covered with black hairs. A yellow to greenish-yellow dye may be produced from the flowers, leaves, and stems. This plant is rather common on stable scree slopes and meadows of the alpine zone and may occasionally be seen along streambeds in the valleys.

Mountain Hollyhock W

Iliamna rivularis MALLOW FAMILY

A stout perennial with stems from 50 to 150 cm high, Mountain Hollyhock closely resembles the cultivated hollyhock grown in gardens. The maple-shaped leaves, which decrease in size upward on the stem, are 3- to 7-lobed with coarsely toothed margins. All green parts of the plant are covered with fine hairs, like tiny silver stars. The leafy stems carry numerous whitish-pink to rose-purple flowers in the leaf axils and on stem tips. These saucer-shaped flowers, up to 6 cm across, are separated by smaller leaves. The fruit is a hairy, globular pod that breaks open like the segments of an orange. Flowering during July and August, this handsome plant is found along highways and stream banks at low elevations.

Marsh Willowherb BKW

Epilobium palustre EVENING PRIMROSE FAMILY

As the common name would suggest, this plant grows in wet places such as bogs or along mossy stream sides. The delicate slender stems, up to 40 cm tall, may be simple or sparingly branched. The paired leaves are oblong-ovate to lance-shaped. A few small, notched flowers, white to pink in colour, droop at the end of the long stalks. The resulting fruit is a capsule 3 to 5 cm long, bearing seeds with a white tuft of hairs. The thread-like stolons issuing from the base of the plant are a useful field mark of the Marsh Willowherb.

Alpine Milkvetch

Mountain Hollyhock

Marsh Willowherb

Spreading Dogbane

BJKWY

Apocynum androsaemifolium

DOGBANE FAMILY

Spreading Dogbane is a shrub 30 to 100 cm tall with freely branching, slender stems. When broken, the leaves and stems exude a milky sap. Bright green above and lighter and somewhat hairy beneath, the leaves are opposite, egg-shaped, with short pointed tips. Characteristically, these leaves droop during the heat of a summer day. Clusters of small, pink, bell-shaped flowers hang from the ends of the leafy stems. The petal lobes are spreading or bent backward and are often streaked with darker pink veins. Red pods, 8 to 10 cm long and filled with many hairy-tipped seeds, replace the sweet-scented flowers. This is a fairly common plant in thickets and wooded areas.

Grouseberry

BJKY

Vaccinium scoparium

HEATH FAMILY

Grouseberry is a low shrub, 10 to 20 cm tall, which often forms a dense ground cover on open mountain slopes near timberline. Its angular branches remain green for several years. The rather small, bright green, oval-shaped leaves, with finely serrated margins, are deciduous. Small urn-shaped flowers hang downward from the leaf axils. These solitary flowers resemble waxen pearls of the softest pink, later turning into small edible berries that are bright coral-red. The juicy berries are attractive to birds, small mammals, and humans.

Dwarf Raspberry; Arctic Raspberry

BJKWY

Rubus arcticus [*R. acaulis*]

ROSE FAMILY

Easy to distinguish from other raspberries by its rose-red flowers and ground-hugging habit, Dwarf Raspberry can be found trailing over moss-covered ground from low elevation bogs to the alpine zone. The flowering stem and tufts of leaves rise from a slender creeping rootstock. From 2 to 5 leaves, divided into 3-parted leaflets with unevenly toothed margins, provide a pleasant contrast to the usually solitary terminal flower and the juicy red berry which follows. The slender pointed sepals are strongly reflexed, and the ribbon-like stamens are a similarly coloured rose-red. The fruits are rather small, but sweet, aromatic, and richly flavoured.

Spreading Dogbane

Grouseberry

Dwarf Raspberry

Prince's Pine; Pipsissewa

BJKWY

Chimaphila umbellata

WINTERGREEN FAMILY

Prince's Pine is a low evergreen plant, 15 to 30 cm tall, with a long creeping rootstock. Its waxy, glossy green leaves are in whorls and have saw-toothed margins. A cluster of 4 to 8 pinkish flowers shaped like small shallow saucers droops gracefully on arching stalks near the tip of the stem. Turn the pleasantly fragrant flower upward and note the 10 stamens radiating like the spokes of a wheel around a fat green ovary. Fruits are roundish capsules, each holding numerous small seeds. The leaves of this plant were used by Indians in a tobacco mixture and as a substitute for tea. Prince's Pine prefers dry, shady coniferous forests.

Red Heather; Red Mountain Heather

BJKWY

Phyllodoce empetriformis

HEATH FAMILY

Thick carpets of this evergreen shrub cover the ground on alpine meadows and thinly wooded slopes near timberline. Clusters of red or reddish-pink, bell-shaped flowers are borne on slender stalks at the stem tips. The sepals surrounding the flowers are a darker red. Leaves are blunt, linear, needle-like, and grooved on both sides; they are more numerous toward the ends of the branches. While not the true heather of Europe, this plant is well known by that name. As you hike in alpine areas, stop a moment and breathe in the subtle perfume from these cheerful bells.

Common Pink Wintergreen

BJKWY

Pyrola asarifolia

WINTERGREEN FAMILY

This is the largest and showiest of the wintergreens in our mountains. The plant has a rosette of basal leaves and a leafless flowering stem that is between 25 and 50 cm tall. The leathery leaves are large, roundish to kidney-shaped, with slightly wavy and sparingly toothed margins. They are a glossy dark green above, often purplish to reddish beneath, with reddish stalks. The leaves retain their colour during winter, thereby giving rise to the name "wintergreen." Up to 20 fragrant flowers crowd the reddish, erect, flowering stem. The flowers are pink to purplish-red, cup-shaped, and each has a style that projects downward like a curved hook. This handsome plant is widespread on stream banks, in open coniferous forests, and occasionally in the lower alpine zone.

Pink Pussytoes; Pink Everlasting

BJKW

Antennaria rosea

COMPOSITE FAMILY

The pastel flush of rosy pink bracts among the many-flowered compact heads makes Pink Pussytoes easy to identify. Its microscopic flowers are hidden in furry down so the flower heads have a fanciful resemblance to tiny pussytoes. This rather handsome species has a rosette of basal leaves, which are covered with woolly white hairs and are somewhat spoon-shaped, with blunt tips. The leaves were used by Indians in smoking mixtures and were also chewed for their flavour. Dried flowers are long-lasting in floral arrangements. This is a common plant which grows in patches on open, dry slopes.

Prince's Pine

Red Heather

Common Pink Wintergreen

Pink Pussytoes

Venus Slipper; Fairy Slipper; Calypso — BJKWY

Calypso bulbosa — ORCHID FAMILY

Venus Slipper is one of the most enchantingly lovely of all the wildflowers within the Canadian Rockies. The drooping blossom of this orchid has a crown of rose-purple sepals and petals, all sharply pointed, twisted, and radiating upwards above the lip. The jewel-like lip or slipper is a wide, whitish apron streaked and spotted with purple and adorned with a cluster of golden hairs. There is a spotted double spur below the lip. The upper lip is broadly winged and also rose-purple. A single leaf, with parallel veins that converge at the tip, appears in the late summer and persists through the winter only to wither and disappear early next summer. Both the leaf and stem grow from an ivory-coloured corm with weak roots that are easily broken. Venus Slipper is generally the earliest orchid to flower in the Rockies. It can be locally common among the mosses in shaded coniferous or aspen forests.

Water Smartweed — BJKW

Polygonum amphibium — BUCKWHEAT FAMILY

Water Smartweed grows from a running rootstock in the water or on the margins of drying ponds in the montane zone. Its leaves are of 2 types: if growing on land, the leaves are lance-like with short petioles; if floating on the water surface, they are waxy and broader with long petioles. This plant has a vast profusion of small, rose-red flowers in erect dense spikes. The small lens-shaped achenes are an important food for ducks.

Mountain Spiraea; Pink Meadowsweet — W

Spiraea densiflora — ROSE FAMILY

A low shrub 50 to 90 cm tall, Mountain Spiraea has dense, flat-topped flower clusters that are a deep rose-pink. The flowers are sweet-scented and have a fluffy appearance because the long stamens intermix with those of adjacent blossoms. Each branch has between 10 and 20 oval leaves 2 to 4 cm long, with rather small marginal teeth except near the base. The chestnut-brown outer bark of the branches peels off in thin, papery layers. Mountain Spiraea is found in wet meadows and other boggy places near timberline.

Grass Pink — W

Dianthus armeria — PINK FAMILY

This annual or biennial, 10 to 50 cm tall, is a European weed which appears to be locally increasing along roadsides and around the stables in Waterton Lakes National Park. The narrowly lance-shaped leaves, almost grass-like, are fused basally around the stem. Pink to red flowers crowd the stem tips. Each petal is attractively spotted and has a shallowly toothed tip. Grass Pink flowers open only briefly during midday, being hidden by long hairy bracts during the remainder of the day.

Venus Slipper

Water Smartweed

Mountain Spiraea

Grass Pink

Alpine Wallflower BJ

Erysimum pallasii MUSTARD FAMILY

The arresting beauty and heavenly fragrance of Alpine Wallflower are more than ample reward for a climb to its rocky habitat high above treeline. Each plant boasts numerous flowers, all a rich purple and cross-shaped. The flowers are on such short stems that they huddle just above the rosette of long, prominently veined, and deeply notched leaves. After fertilization the flowering stems elongate to between 15 and 30 cm and carry long, curved, purple seed pods well above the leaves.

Purple Saxifrage BJKY

Saxifraga oppositifolia SAXIFRAGE FAMILY

While other saxifrages in our area are dressed in flowers of white or yellow, this saxifrage alone is garbed with flowers of the richest rose-purple to royal purple. Each stem produces a solitary, star-shaped flower on a short stalk at the end of the stem. However, the mat of tightly packed leafy stems, each with its own flower, may result in such a mass of bloom that the tiny leaves are nearly concealed. The crimped petals, accented by brownish-orange anthers, are narrowed to a blunt tip. Overlapping, scale-like leaves, ranked in fours and with hairy margins, distinguish this saxifrage from Moss Campion, which is found in similar habitats. Look for carpets of these charming flowers above timberline, on meadows, and on scree slopes soon after snow-release.

Moss Campion BJKWY

Silene acaulis PINK FAMILY

Moss Campion is a perfect example of a plant adapted to withstand the fierce winds, intense sunshine, and extreme temperatures of the alpine region. These plants sometimes extend in tight cushions for nearly a metre over rock and thin topsoil. The bright green mats, looking like patches of moss, are spangled with flowers that vary from pale to bright pink to lavender (rarely white). They can be found from June through August, depending on the elevation. The small, 5-lobed tubular flowers appear to project from the mats without stems. The flowers are scented to attract night-flying insects, which cross-fertilize them. From up close the sharp-pointed leaves resemble conifer needles.

Alpine Wallflower

Purple Saxifrage

Moss Campion

Bearberry; Kinnikinnick BJKWY

Arctostaphylos uva-ursi HEATH FAMILY

This trailing or matted evergreen shrub has long branches with brownish-red, flaky bark and shiny green, leathery, oval leaves. Drooping urn-shaped flowers, pale pink in colour, are at the ends of the stems. The dull red berries are edible, but they are dry and mealy. They are relished by bears and birds and were eaten by the Indians in several different ways. Kinnikinnick, one of the common names for the plant, is an Indian word meaning "something to smoke"; the dried leaves were used as tobacco or mixed with it. The plant was also used in a tanning mixture and as a dye. Bearberry is common and widespread on gravel terraces, in coniferous woods, and on alpine slopes.

Alpine Lousewort BJ

Pedicularis arctica FIGWORT FAMILY

In the Rocky Mountains, this plant is restricted to the high alpine. One to several stems arise from a stout, almost white taproot. Small fern-like leaves grow from the base and extend over the whole length of the flowering stem, and both leaves and stems are covered with woolly hairs. Beautiful rose-purple, 2-lipped flowers are closely set along the elongated stem. The prominently arching upper lip of the corolla tube has a pair of sharp teeth near the tip, while the shorter, lower lip is 3-lobed.

Northern Laurel; Bog Laurel BJKW

Kalmia polifolia HEATH FAMILY

This is a small evergreen shrub, usually less than 20 cm tall, with pink to rose-purple, saucer-shaped flowers that are borne in clusters at the end of red stalks. The showy flowers have 10 arched filaments, each bent and held in a crease in the corolla. At the slightest touch by an insect, the anthers snap inward and dust the visitor with a shower of golden pollen, thus ensuring cross-pollination when the insect moves to other flowers. The dark green, leathery leaves are rolled under along the margins and have a whitish lower surface. They contain andromedotoxin, which is poisonous to livestock. Grey and yellow dyes can be produced from the leaves. Look for this gorgeous plant in wet meadows, swampy places, and especially in peat bogs.

Bearberry

Bearberry

Alpine Lousewort

Northern Laurel

Prickly Rose

BJKWY

Rosa acicularis

ROSE FAMILY

Prickly Rose, the floral emblem of Alberta, is the best known and most easily recognized of all the flowering shrubs in our region. Its sweet-scented, open-faced flowers, 3 to 6 cm across, are bright pink or reddish-pink. The flower has 5 sepals and 5 somewhat heart-shaped petals surrounding a shower of yellow-gold stamens. The plant's alternate leaves are composed of 3 to 7 leaflets, which are thin, green, and lightly toothed. Many slender prickles arm the stems, which are 50 to 125 cm tall. Framed in a background of green leaves, the flower's glory is replaced in late summer by the scarlet, globose to pear-shaped fruits (rose hips). These remain on the stem throughout the winter, providing food for numerous birds and mammals. Rose hips are unusually high in vitamins A and C and can be made into jam, jelly, syrup, marmalade, and juice. Indians employed the leaves for tea and in salads, and the inner bark for smoking. The petals can be used to make a perfume or dried for a sachet. At one time the dried fruits served as beads for necklaces. This species hybridizes freely with another common and very similar species, Common Wild Rose (*R. woodsii*), and hybridization between the two makes identification difficult. Both grow on dry grassy slopes, open woods, roadsides, and river banks almost to timberline.

Red Monkey Flower

JW

Mimulus lewisii

FIGWORT FAMILY

Favourite habitats of Red Monkey Flower are near ice-cold mountain streams or other open wet places at moderate elevations. In such habitats the plant, with its luxuriant dark green foliage and showers of glowing rose-red flowers, may grow in solid masses. The clasping leaves are conspicuously veined with widely spaced teeth along the margins. Showy flowers grow on long stalks from the axils of the upper leaves. A round, 2-lipped, funnel-shaped corolla is formed by the 5 lobes. The lower 3-lobed lip has a hairy throat, handsomely marked with deep yellow. Short sticky hairs cover the whole plant. Bees and hummingbirds are frequently attracted to these flowers.

Prickly Rose

Prickly Rose

Red Monkey Flower

Leafy Aster BJKWY

Aster subspicatus [*A. foliaceus*] COMPOSITE FAMILY

Leafy Aster is a highly variable plant, making description difficult. The slender stems, from 30 to 100 cm tall, are greenish to purplish and glabrous to pubescent. Leaves may be slightly toothed or entire, and are oblanceolate with petioles on the lower stem but lanceolate without petioles towards the tip. The flower heads, 2 or 3 cm across, have blue to rosy-purple ray flowers and yellowish disk flowers. Their outer involucral bracts are broad and leafy. These plants may reproduce by rhizomes or seeds. Like several other asters, they flower from late summer until killed by autumn frosts. This widespread plant's favoured habitats are moist open woods and stream banks to near timberline.

Dwarf Canadian Primrose; Bird's-Eye Primrose BJKY

Primula mistassinica PRIMROSE FAMILY

Making up in beauty what it lacks in size, Dwarf Canadian Primrose is a small, delicate, but showy species that likes moist situations such as stream margins and wet meadows. Its leafless flowering stem, growing from a rosette of small, minutely toothed, oval leaves, is only 10 to 15 cm tall. A small open cluster of flowers is set at the top of the stem. Each flower looks like a miniature pinwheel with 5 deeply notched pink petals and a contrasting yellow eye. On occasion, the petals may be lilac or white. The short-capsuled fruits are often covered by dried sepals.

Roseroot BJKW

Sedum rosea [*Tolmachevia integrifolia*] STONECROP FAMILY

Roseroot is a rare alpine plant growing in moist rocky or gravelly sites. It is a perennial with a branching rootstock, each branch producing a leafy annual stem from 5 to 15 cm tall. The leaves are succulent, egg-shaped to oblong, and may have smooth or toothed margins. Flowers are in flat-topped clusters with the central flower of each cluster blooming first. The male and female flowers may be on different parts of the flower cluster. Male flowers are yellow or purple, while the female flowers are always purple. Petals of the flowers are nearly twice as long as the sepals. The seed pods are plump, erect, and reddish-purple. When young, the succulent stems and leaves are edible as salad or potherb.

Leafy Aster

Dwarf Canadian Primrose

Roseroot

Common Fireweed; Great Willowherb BJKWY

Epilobium angustifolium EVENING PRIMROSE FAMILY

In disturbed sites, such as along roadways or in burned-over forests, a galaxy of large, magenta (rarely white) flowers of this plant is likely to brighten the way during the summer. The flowers open from the bottom upward to the top of the spike, on a plant which is often up to 2 m high. Seed pods, mature flowers, and buds may all be present on a spike at the same time. This perennial has large, dark green, lance-like leaves, which are paler and veiny underneath. The seed pods are long and slender and produce numerous seeds with tufts of silky hairs for carrying them long distances in a breeze. The plant has several food uses: young shoots may be cooked like asparagus; young leaves, peeled stems, and buds may be added to salads or cooked in soup and stews; tea can be brewed from older leaves and flowers. This plant colonizes burned areas rapidly and helps control erosion. Common Fireweed is the floral emblem of the Yukon Territory.

Mountain Fireweed; River Beauty BJKWY

Epilobium latifolium EVENING PRIMROSE FAMILY

Mountain Fireweed resembles Common Fireweed in general appearance but it has shorter stems, generally less than 40 cm, broader leaves, and larger, more brilliantly coloured flowers. The stems bear waxy, bluish-green, lance-shaped leaves with rounded tips. The flower parts are in fours—4 sepals, 4 pink to rose-purple petals, a deeply 4-lobed white style, and 8 stamens. Long, narrow capsules contain many tiny seeds, each with silken fluff attached, to be borne away by the wind until they find some favoured niche. Flowers and buds of the plant may be eaten raw as a salad; its young leaves, when cooked, are an excellent substitute for spinach. The plant is also cooling and astringent and was used to promote healing of wounds; in powdered form it was used to stop hemorrhages. Yellow to green dye can be produced from the flowers. Mountain Fireweed grows as a pioneer, often in dense colonies, on gravelly floodplains and river bars where the blue-green of the dense leaves and the waving masses of brilliantly coloured flowers often obscure the stony ground beneath.

Sticky Purple Geranium BKW

Geranium viscosissimum GERANIUM FAMILY

Sticky Purple Geranium, 30 to 60 cm high, blooms profusely for much of the summer. The flowers with their large, showy, rose-purple petals, strongly veined with purple, demand attention over their less strikingly garbed companions. The long-petioled leaves, deeply lobed and split into 5 to 7 sharply toothed divisions, are in opposite pairs along the stem. Sticky, glandular hairs cover the stems, leaves, and some flower parts. The seed capsule elongates into a long beak as it ripens, and eventually splits lengthways from the bottom up into 5 divisions, shooting the seeds away from the parent plant. Although most at home in the light shade of aspen groves, Sticky Purple Geranium also grows in exposed grasslands.

Common Fireweed

Mountain Fireweed

Sticky Purple Geranium

Striped Coralroot

BJKWY

Corallorhiza striata

ORCHID FAMILY

These plants lack chlorophyll and therefore cannot manufacture their own food. They are parasites on the fungi that live among pine and spruce needles in coniferous forests. They do not have proper roots, but part of the stem is underground, where its short, thick fibres branch and interweave in a manner reminiscent of coral. Striped Coralroot is the most striking member of its genus. Erect purple or yellow-brown stems, 15 to 40 cm high, terminate in a raceme of 10 to 25 large drooping flowers. The petals and sepals may be pinkish, yellowish, or nearly white, with 3 conspicuous stripes of deep red-purple. The lower petal or lip is broader and its stripes join into a solid purple, tongue-shaped tip.

Mountain Sorrel

BJKWY

Oxyria digyna

BUCKWHEAT FAMILY

Mountain Sorrel forms dense rosettes with clusters of long-petioled, kidney-shaped, green and somewhat succulent leaves; there are several short upright leaves on each branched stem. The ends of the stems bear short sprays of rather insignificant green flowers. They are replaced in mid-summer by prominently winged, bright red fruits, whose colour is from the enlarged sepals which form thin, papery envelopes around each seed. They dangle from a slender stem and quiver in the wind like a Japanese lantern. In exposed alpine sites the whole plant often turns dark reddish-green. The leaves are good sources of vitamins A and C; they may be used in salads and as a potherb in soup. This plant can reduce the itching of mosquito bites, and it produces a yellowish-green dye. Caribou, marmots, and pikas eat the leaves and stems, and lemmings like the fleshy roots. The leaves have a refreshingly sharp taste. Mountain Sorrel is a plant of the alpine region, particularly along streams, seepages, and crevices.

Bracted Lousewort; Wood Betony

BJKWY

Pedicularis bracteosa

FIGWORT FAMILY

Bracted Lousewort is an unmistakable plant because of its stiffly erect, purplish stem, naked near the bottom; its dense spike of arching tubular flowers; and its fern-like leaves. The stem, 40 to 100 cm tall, arises from a thick, perennial rootstock and is devoid of leaves on the lower third. Much-dissected leaves grow from the upper portion of the stem until they merge into bracts, which are interspersed with flowers in a dense terminal spike. Both the upper stem and leaves are bronze or wine-tinged. Individual flowers are yellow, often tinged with red or purple, and are curved downward at the tip. The corolla is distinctly 2-lipped. The upper lip is long and flattened at the sides and arched at the apex, cupping over the stamens; the lower lip is shorter, 3-parted, and toothed, and it curves in so much that it nearly closes the throat. You may fancy that the flowers almost resemble small parrots' bills peeping out from among the bracts. Look for Bracted Lousewort in moist soils in open woods and alpine meadows.

Striped Coralroot

Mountain Sorrel

Bracted Lousewort

Western Wood Lily — BJKWY

Lilium philadelphicum — LILY FAMILY

The floral emblem of Saskatchewan, this strikingly beautiful lily may be up to 0.5 m or more in height and has an upright flower with petals of orange or orange-red at the top of the stem. The petals are narrowly tapered and become golden toward the base while the inner basal portion is spotted with a maroon-wine colour. The flowers, which may be 6 to 10 cm across, are generally solitary but occasionally plants with 5 or more blooms are encountered. The leaves are narrow, pointed, and whorled. The egg-shaped fruit is 2 to 4 cm long, containing numerous flat seeds. The plant springs from a thick, scaly bulb. It is found in a variety of habitats from grasslands to open woodlands, usually at low elevations. Unfortunately, Western Wood Lily is often picked, and as a result it has disappeared from some localities.

Red-flowered Columbine; Western Columbine — JY

Aquilegia formosa — BUTTERCUP FAMILY

This graceful plant displays the regal beauty of its bloom above the fern-like foliage of its leaves. The daintily suspended flowers have 5 coral-red, wing-shaped sepals and 5 tube-shaped, yellow petals, each flaring at the open end and tapering to an orange-red spur at the other. Butterflies and hummingbirds are attracted by the vivid splash of flower colour and by the nectar within the spurs. A central tuft of stamens and styles protrudes like a brush, to deliver and receive pollen from the visiting birds and insects. The plant's leaves are compound, long-stalked, and divided into many segments. Many seeds are borne in a head of 5 pods, which are erect at maturity. Favoured habitats for the Red-flowered Columbine are open woods and valleys as well as moist alpine and subalpine meadows.

False Huckleberry; False Azalea — BJKWY

Menziesia ferruginea [*M. glabella*] — HEATH FAMILY

This much-branched deciduous shrub may form thickets up to 2 m tall, particularly in cool, moist forests of the subalpine zone. The pale green leaves have wavy margins and grow in clusters alternately along the stems. Small salmon-coloured to greenish-orange flowers hang by short stalks in drooping clusters beneath the leaves. The 4-lobed corolla is urn-shaped, while the 4 short but broad sepals are greenish and fringed with hairs. All of the above-ground parts of the plant are generally covered with rusty coloured glands. While in flower False Huckleberry may be confused with Huckleberry, but the latter produces luscious berries while the former, alas, produces only an inedible 4-parted pod, which becomes erect as it ripens. This shrub is attractive in the autumn when its leaves turn a brilliant crimson-orange.

Western Wood Lily

Red-flowered Columbine

False Huckleberry

Purple & Blue Flowers

Prairie Crocus; Pasque Flower

BJKWY

Anemone patens

BUTTERCUP FAMILY

As harbingers of early spring, the blooms of the Prairie Crocus emerge from the ground before its leaves have developed, often before the snow has melted. The cup-shaped flowers, in varying colours from royal purple to bluish-lavender and occasionally white, often paint entire hillsides in the grasslands and open woods. These 6-parted flowers are often a paler colour inside than outside, and they enclose a cluster of bright yellow stamens. The deeply cleft leaves and the stems, cloaked in an army of silky white hairs, develop after the flowers appear. In time the flowers are replaced by a wad of achenes, each with a long, feathery tail. This conspicuous and lovely plant is the floral emblem of Manitoba and the state flower of South Dakota.

Purple Onion; Wild Chives

BJKWY

Allium schoenoprasum

LILY FAMILY

Allium contains so many beautiful species that it should not be condemned for a smell which is never offensive unless the plants are roughly handled. Purple Onion has a densely clustered head of showy blossoms at the end of each stem. They are rose to purplish-pink, with darker veins. Both the straight, stout flowering stems and hollow cylindrical leaves spring from a pink to purple bulb with a white membranous coat. The edible bulb has a strong, hot flavour. Our garden chives were derived from this wild species. This handsome bright-flowered onion may be found in damp open habitats from low elevations to timberline.

Wild Mint; Field Mint

BJKWY

Mentha arvensis

MINT FAMILY

As in other members of the Mint family, this plant has irregular flowers, square stems, and opposite leaves. The leaves are egg- or lance-shaped with glandular dots on both surfaces. They are pointed at the tips and have teeth on the margins. The simple or sparsely branched stems are covered with hair. Crowded whorls of light pink or purple flowers stud several of the upper leaf axils. The upper flower lobe is notched and is usually broader than the 3 others. Four stamens and 2-lobed pistils project well beyond the mouth of the flower tube. Bruise a few leaves and note the very aromatic menthol fragrance. The leaves were used by Indians for flavouring meat and pemmican and as a refreshing tea. Typical habitats for Wild Mint include wet woods, stream banks, and lakeshores.

Prairie Crocus

Prairie Crocus

Purple Onion

Wild Mint

Selfheal; Healall

BJKWY

Prunella vulgaris

MINT FAMILY

Selfheal has all the typical characteristics of the mint family: square stem, opposite leaves, and 2-lipped flowers. The upper lip is arched or hooded; the lower is 3-parted, with the middle part much larger, and attractively fringed with white hairs. The flowers are generally purplish-blue, rarely pink or white. The calyx, usually purplish-green, is covered with long hairs. Small brownish-green, bract-like leaves are interspersed among the flowers in the thick terminal spike. As suggested by the common names, the plant was once esteemed for healing wounds. A refreshing beverage can be made by chopping and boiling the leaves. This attractive plant is fairly common in damp fields and woods in the montane zone.

Woollen Breeches; Dwarf Waterleaf

W

Hydrophyllum capitatum

WATERLEAF FAMILY

After the long winter, Woollen Breeches is among the first harbingers of spring. The purplish-blue to white flowers grow in a dense head or ball-like cluster. The individual flowers are cup-shaped, with both anthers and 2-lobed stigmas extended well beyond the corolla. The whole plant is loosely hairy and the sepals are bristly. Each flower cluster is generally overtopped, and sometimes hidden, by a small leaf. Most of the leaves have long petioles and form a basal cluster. Each of the 5 to 11 segmented leaflets ends in a sharply pointed tip. This unusual and very attractive plant is found in moist woods and on shaded slopes in the southern portion of the Canadian Rockies.

Wild Bergamont; Horsemint

W

Monarda fistulosa

MINT FAMILY

Bright patches of Wild Bergamont flaunt their showy flowers in grasslands and open woods during late July and August. This perennial, with stiffly erect, square stems 30 to 70 cm tall, has a strong and distinctive minty odour. Each stem is topped by a dense cluster of pink to lilac flowers. The petals, about 3 cm long, are deeply cleft into narrow upper and lower lips that open wide at the mouth. Two stamens and a pistil extend beyond the lips. The sepals are fused into a narrow tube, which is crowded with dense white hairs. Both petals and sepals are marked with glandular dots. The opposite, strongly toothed, grey-green leaves are triangular-ovate in shape and pointed at the tip. Wild Bergamont was reported to be used by Indians to relieve acne, bronchial complaints, and stomach pains.

Showy Locoweed

BJWY

Oxytropis splendens

PEA FAMILY

An attractive legume, Showy Locoweed has silvery, silky leaves growing from a branched woody base. Each leaf is comprised of numerous leaflets. The flower stalks generally elongate to hold dense clusters of 10 to 35 flowers above the silvery foliage. The flowers are blue to reddish-purple, drying to violet. Individual flowers are 1 to 2 cm long, with a densely hairy calyx about half that length. This boldly handsome plant is widely distributed throughout low-elevation grasslands.

Selfheal

Woollen Breeches

Wild Bergamont

Showy Locoweed

Inflated Oxytrope; Bladder Locoweed — BJKWY

Oxytropis podocarpa — PEA FAMILY

This pretty little alpine plant usually grows from a rosette of leaves that lies flat on the ground, spreading out from the stout taproot. The leaves are 2 to 5 cm long and consist of between 9 and 25 tiny, linear leaflets which are covered with silky hairs. The leafless stalks, barely overtopping the leaves, terminate with up to 3 flowers (most commonly with 2) about 2 cm long. Each pale purple, pea-like flower has a dark purple, hairy calyx. The characteristic beak of the keel, formed from the 2 lowermost fused petals, is distinctive and will distinguish an *Oxytropis* from an *Astragalus* (Milkvetch). More spectacular than the flowers are the inflated pods, 2 to 3 cm long, which turn bright red to purple in autumn; these pods are egg-shaped, with a style that remains attached. The seeds within the fat pods are eaten by various insects and small mammals. Inflated Oxytrope is a plant of windblown, gravelly slopes and ridges high above timberline.

Siberian Aster; Arctic Aster — BJKWY

Aster sibiricus — COMPOSITE FAMILY

The stems of this plant are often purplish, arising singly or in clusters from a creeping rhizome. The leaves are highly variable, but they are generally lance-shaped, hairy beneath but smooth above, with serrated margins. Broad-faced, lavender-blue to purple ray flowers are emphasized by a central boss of closely packed, tiny yellow disk flowers. The involucral bracts are mostly green with purple margins and white hairs. Although basically an alpine plant, Siberian Aster can be found on gravelly river flats and other rocky areas.

Inflated Oxytrope

Inflated Oxytrope

Siberian Aster

Elephanthead

BJWY

Pedicularis groenlandica

FIGWORT FAMILY

Have you seen any miniature pink elephants lately? Perhaps you are only seeing a flower of this plant with its amazing likeness to an elephant's head with a high forehead, big ears, long upraised trunk, and small tusks. The upper lip of the corolla resembles the head and upturned trunk, 2 petals of the lower lip form the ears, and the central lobe is the mouth. These purple-pink flowers are arranged at the top of a rather compact spike, which may be up to 50 cm tall. The leaves are deeply divided and fern-like. Both the leaves and stems are often tinged with purple. The carrot-like roots may be eaten raw or cooked in soup. Elephanthead is conspicuous in wet meadows and marshes.

Shooting Star

BJKWY

Dodecatheon pulchellum [*D. radicatum*]

PRIMROSE FAMILY

Pulchellum means "beautiful" and the name is certainly appropriate as the varied pink to lilac-purple colours of the flowers are unusually lovely. Clusters of such nodding flowers grow from the tip of the flowering stem, which varies from 10 to 20 cm in height. The petals bend back and are often more intensely coloured near the base, which is ringed with deep yellow and trimmed with a zigzag of rose-purple. The dark green basal leaves are erect and lance-shaped, with the broadest part toward the tip. As the brown seed capsules ripen, they assume an upright position, thus aiding in the dispersal of the seeds. Shooting Stars can be very abundant in moist meadows, the flowers producing waves of colour from June through July, depending on the elevation.

Northern Sweetvetch

BJKWY

Hedysarum boreale [*H. mackenzii*]

PEA FAMILY

Northern Sweetvetch is a low, bushy perennial, up to 50 cm tall, whose unusual seed pods look like short strings of flat beads rigidly joined to each other. The constrictions between each seed in the pod are a useful characteristic to distinguish hedysarums from milkvetches and locoweeds, which have similar flowers, but pods shaped more like those of garden peas. Short grey hairs cover the 9 to 13 leaflets, which are elliptical to almost egg-shaped. Each leafy stem ends in a crowded cluster of large, rose-purple, pea-shaped flowers, which are sweet-scented. The lower petal, or keel, has a distinctive shape like the forepart of a boat. Grizzly bears eat the roots and often make large excavations in their quest for these delicacies. When Northern Sweetvetch forms large colonies on grassy slopes or on well-watered gravel flats, the rousing colour of the blossoms is a delight to the eye.

Elephanthead

Shooting Star

Northern Sweetvetch

Kittentails BW

Besseya wyomingensis FIGWORT FAMILY

This small perennial, 15 to 30 cm tall, is covered with fine white hairs on all green parts. The lance-shaped basal leaves have long petioles and toothed margins, whereas the stem leaves are much smaller and lack petioles, clasping the stem directly. The flowers consist of 2 or 3 green sepals, no petals, 2 deep purple stamens, and a purple style with a button-like stigma. The flowers are in a dense spike, with numerous small green bracts. The name Kittentails is derived from the halo-like cluster of long purple stamens. These showy flowers add a splash of colour to grasslands and alpine slopes in the early summer.

Few-flowered Milkvetch BJW

Astragalus vexilliflexus PEA FAMILY

Growing from a thick taproot, Few-flowered Milkvetch is a profusely branching plant which is mat-like and seldom more than 20 cm tall. Each leaf has 7 to 13 leaflets, which are sharply tipped and lance-shaped. All green parts of the plant are thinly haired. From 2 to 10 flowers cluster along the stem on short stalks. The petals are deep lavender-purple (rarely white). Although most common on dry alpine slopes, this plant is also found at lower elevations on eroded and otherwise disturbed areas.

Creeping Beardtongue BKWY

Penstemon ellipticus FIGWORT FAMILY

There are more than 100 species of *Penstemon* in North America, of which at least 12 occur in the southern Canadian Rocky Mountains. Of those, Creeping Beardtongue is one of the most handsome and conspicuous. Its large trumpet-shaped flowers, pink to lilac-purple and mostly less than 3 cm long, may be so numerous that they form a mass of brilliant colour which obscures the leaves and prostrate stems. The corolla tube is 2-lipped; the lower lip is ornamented with 2 folds and long white hairs. Of the 5 stamens, 1 is sterile with a long yellow beard that protrudes at the widened throat. After the corolla falls, the egg-shaped brown capsule begins to mature. These plants are dwarf shrubs from 10 to 20 cm tall, with trailing leafy stems. They are semi-evergreen, some of the leaves turning red and dropping in the autumn. The leaves are opposite, ovate, and up to 3 cm long. Cushions of this flower-bedecked shrub may be found on dry rocky slopes in the subalpine and alpine zones.

Kittentails

Few-flowered Milkvetch

Creeping Beardtongue

Tall Purple Fleabane; Mountain Erigeron

BJKWY

Erigeron peregrinus

COMPOSITE FAMILY

Stems of this very charming perennial grow 30 to 70 cm high from a thick rootstock. Basal leaves are petioled and narrow, broadening toward their apex, while the stem leaves are smaller and stalkless. The winsome flower, resembling that of a daisy, has a yellow centre of disk florets with a surrounding circle of between 30 and 80 deep rose-purple (sometimes pale pink or even white) ray florets. The large flower heads are usually solitary, but smaller heads occasionally develop from the axils of the upper leaves. The involucral bracts are long, pointed, and usually green. Characteristics of the involucral bracts are important in distinguishing fleabanes from asters: bracts of fleabanes are uniform in length and arranged in 1 or 2 slightly overlapping rings while the bracts of asters are shingled and the outer ones are shorter than the inner ones. Tall Purple Fleabane is common in damp subalpine and alpine meadows.

Four-parted Gentian; Felwort

BJKWY

Gentiana propinqua [*Gentianella propinqua*]

GENTIAN FAMILY

This annual is quite variable in size and structure. At lower elevations it may branch from the base and have 10 to 12 flowers on pedicels from the upper leaf axils, whereas flowering stems in exposed alpine situations are short and unbranched. The stems are often purplish, and the leaves are lance-shaped and entire. The flower at the end of the stem, always the largest, is about 2 cm long with a blue to pale-violet corolla, which fades with age. Corolla tubes, which open only slightly at the top, are divided into 4 lobes, a characteristic that gives rise to one of the popular names, Four-parted Gentian.

Parry's Townsendia

BJW

Townsendia parryi

COMPOSITE FAMILY

Blooming early in the spring, the showy flower heads of Parry's Townsendia hug the ground, directly above a very short stem. The central disk flowers are deep yellow, surrounded by broad ray flowers of violet to bluish-purple. The stems, spoon-shaped leaves, and involucral bracts are covered with stiff white hairs. Most of the leaves form a rosette at ground level. You may find this attractive plant in rocky or grassy places from low elevations to the alpine zone, but if you wait until all the snow is gone, you will miss the flowers.

Alpine Rockcress

BJKWY

Arabis lyallii

MUSTARD FAMILY

The taproot of this small alpine gem may give rise to a variable number of stems. The basal leaves have petioles of about the same length as their lance-shaped blades while smaller leaves clasp the stem. A few cross-shaped flowers, with 4 purplish or rose-coloured petals, are borne at the tip of short stems. After flowering, the upper stem continues to grow as the stiffly erect and sharply pointed seed pods mature. Alpine Rockcress may be found on exposed rocky ridges and herbmats above timberline.

Tall Purple Fleabane

Four-parted Gentian

Parry's Townsendia

Alpine Rockcress

Jacob's Ladder BJKW

Polemonium pulcherrimum PHLOX FAMILY

Pulcherrimum means "very handsome" and that is indeed an apt description for this beautiful perennial. It is a tufted plant, 5 to 25 cm tall, with sparingly branched stems. The fern-like leaves are mostly basal, each with 11 to 23 leaflets; there are a few reduced leaves on the stem. These leaflets are so evenly spaced that the leaves look like miniature ladders, thereby giving rise to the popular name. Pale to dark cobalt-blue, cup-shaped flowers, with a vivid orangish-yellow ring at the base, are borne in an open cluster. The brilliant cascade of blossoms entices bees to settle and collect nectar while leaving pollen from another flower. Jacob's Ladder grows in open, well-drained sites from the montane zone to just above timberline. Enjoy it out-of-doors to avoid its unpleasant odour.

Sky Pilot; Skunkweed W

Polemonium viscosum PHLOX FAMILY

Sky Pilot is a strikingly handsome alpine plant of exposed scree slopes. Its closely packed leaves are short and consist of numerous roundish, 3- to 5-parted leaflets, which are unpleasantly sticky to handle and have a heavy odour suggestive of skunk. The flower clusters are dense and rounded. Their funnel-shaped corollas have 5 expanded lobes, a circle of 5 stamens, and a long thread-like style. The orange pollen of the stamens contrasts with the brilliantly blue petals. Despite the offensive odour of the leaves, the flowers are sweet-scented.

Silky Scorpionweed; Mountain Phacelia BJKWY

Phacelia sericea WATERLEAF FAMILY

The flowers of Silky Scorpionweed, a plant up to 50 cm high, are densely clustered on a spike. Their intense violet-blue petals are accented by the long violet filaments of the stamens and the brilliant orange anthers. All this contrasts sharply with the silvery leaves, which are divided into many narrow sections. The stems and leaves are covered with silvery, silky hairs, which make the setting of the long-stemmed flower spike all the more striking. This perennial graces open slopes, screes, and rock crevices at high altitudes.

Sawwort; Purple Hawkweed BJKY

Saussurea nuda [*S. densa*] COMPOSITE FAMILY

A sturdy mountain dweller, Sawwort is found on rocky alpine slopes at medium to high altitudes. At first glance it looks like a deformed thistle. Its thistle-like flower heads are like tight balls of wool, from which protrude beautiful, dark bluish-purple disk florets. They are so densely clustered at the top of the short stem that the large, densely furred, saw-edged leaves are almost obscured. Sawwort stands 10 to 20 cm tall and is quite a giant in comparison with many of its floral companions on the rocky slopes where it grows. After a strenuous climb to its habitat, stop to rest and discover the pleasant fragrance of this flower.

Jacob's Ladder

Sky Pilot

Silky Scorpionweed

Sawwort

Blue Beardtongue

BWY

Penstemon albertinus

FIGWORT FAMILY

Blue Beardtongue grows in tufts 10 to 30 cm tall. Arranged in an open cluster around the upper part of the stem, the bright blue to purplish flowers are tubular in shape and 2-lipped. Each petal tube is sparsely hairy outside with long white and yellow hairs inside the lower throat. One of the 5 stamens is sterile and densely bearded. The petioled, basal leaves are egg- to lance-shaped with inconspicuous teeth on the margins; the stem leaves lack petioles and are lance-shaped with shallowly toothed margins, growing opposite each other along the stem. This attractive plant with its spires of azure flowers is fairly common in dry, open habitats at low to middle elevations.

Slender Beardtongue

BJW

Penstemon procerus

FIGWORT FAMILY

Slender Beardtongue is nearly identical in appearance and size to Yellow Beardtongue except for its deep purplish-blue (rarely pinkish to white) flowers. It can be distinguished from Blue Beardtongue by its rather crowded cluster of small flowers in contrast to the open arrangement of slightly larger flowers for the latter. The flowers may be in a dense cluster, as illustrated, or in several crowded whorls (see Yellow Beardtongue). Sharply ovate blades on long petioles form a basal rosette of leaves; there are a few stem leaves without petioles. Usually rather common, this plant may be found in open forests to timberline.

Silky Lupine

W

Lupinus sericeus

PEA FAMILY

Highly variable, Silky Lupine is a common plant within the southern limits of our area. Meadows and forest openings may be blued with its flowers from late June to early August. It is a perennial herb, 40 to 80 cm tall, often growing in dense clumps or bunches. The leaves consist of 5 to 9 very narrow leaflets with densely silky hairs on both sides. Blue to bluish-purple flowers cluster along the top third of the stem. The standard is densely hairy on the back. The pods are 2 or 3 cm long and contain 4 to 6 seeds. Alkaloids in the seeds may be poisonous, particularly to sheep. Nodules on the roots of this legume contain nitrogen-fixing bacteria which enrich the soil.

Blue Beardtongue

Slender Beardtongue

Silky Lupine

Bull Thistle

BWY

Cirsium vulgare

COMPOSITE FAMILY

Another Eurasian introduction, Bull Thistle is a much-hated but interesting weed. It is a stout-stemmed biennial, 50 to 150 cm tall, with an armour of sharp prickles. The dark green, hairy leaves are deeply cleft and very prickly. Numerous rose-purple flower heads, resembling shaving brushes, develop at the ends of the branches. The involucral bracts are cobwebby, each with a spreading yellow spine tip. This thistle is found along roadsides and other disturbed places.

Common Butterwort

BJKWY

Pinguicula vulgaris

BLADDERWORT FAMILY

The beautiful violet-purple, irregularly shaped flowers of Common Butterwort are on leafless stalks up to 10 cm high. The calyx is notched into 3 upper and 2 lower lobes, forming a funnel-like structure. The spur is whitish to dark in colour with short hairs. Pale green leaves press close to the ground and overlap one another in a basal rosette. Common Butterwort is one of the few carnivorous plants in the Canadian Rockies. Its yellowish-green, thickened leaves, with rolled-in edges, exude a sticky substance that attracts, ensnares, and digests tiny insects, enabling the plant to obtain nitrogen and other nutrients. The insect-catching and digestive powers of this plant help compensate for the lack of nutrients in the ecological niche in which it grows. This intriguing plant may be found in bogs, on wet rocky banks, and on mossy stream sides, mainly in valleys at low elevation.

Stickseed

BKW

Hackelia floribunda [*Lappula floribunda*]

BORAGE FAMILY

A hairy biennial or short-lived perennial, Stickseed has stiffly erect stems up to 1 m tall. Near the top they support several loose clusters of yellow-centred, blue flowers on curving stalks. Each corolla has a short tubular section which abruptly spreads into 5 lobes. The pistil later produces 4 small nutlets with rows of hooked prickles, which readily adhere to clothing, fur, or hair, thereby giving rise to the common name. Moist meadows and woodlands, thickets, and stream banks are likely habitats in which to search for this plant.

Blue Camas

W

Camassia quamash

LILY FAMILY

The onion-like bulbs of Blue Camas were a very important food plant for Indians, trappers, and early settlers. They were baked, boiled, roasted, or eaten raw; they were made into a molasses and into "Camas" pie, or ground into flour for bread. So important were the bulbs that local Indian wars were fought over the rights to certain large meadows containing the plant. Arising from the bulbs are rather stout stems 30 to 60 cm tall, with long, narrow, grass-like leaves about two-thirds as long as the naked stem. The startling blue to purplish-blue flowers have 6 separate, but similar, petals and sepals, which are spreading and somewhat unevenly spaced. These segments contrast vividly with the 6 golden stamens. Flowering in June, Blue Camas grows in wet meadows and along stream banks in the southern portion of our area.

Bull Thistle

Common Butterwort

Stickseed

Blue Camas

Low Larkspur

BKW

Delphinium bicolor

BUTTERCUP FAMILY

Growing from prairie meadows to alpine ridges, this strikingly handsome plant blooms from May to July, depending on the elevation. It arises from somewhat fleshy roots, its stems 15 to 35 cm tall with deeply cut leaflets that are chiefly basal. From 3 to 12 flowers are borne in a loose spike. Each of the 4 lower sepals is intense blue-purple in colour, widely flared, and appreciably larger than the upper sepal, which extends backward into a prominent hollow spur. Smaller than the sepals, the 4 petals are of two kinds: the lower 2 petals are dark blue and hairy and the upper 2, even smaller, are creamy white with purple veins, when fresh. The mature fruit is an erect cluster of pods about 2 cm long, containing many seeds. Low Larkspur is poisonous to cattle, particularly in the early spring; the leaves contain several toxic alkaloids, including delphinine. Curiously, sheep are unaffected by the alkaloids and they have been used to eradicate the plant in some pastures. While not common, Low Larkspur may be locally abundant.

Alpine Speedwell; Alpine Veronica

BJKWY

Veronica wormskjoldii [*V. alpina*]

FIGWORT FAMILY

This perennial alpine beauty is easily recognized. It has a flattened, usually 4-petalled corolla, with only 2 stamens and a pistil. The corolla is less than 1 cm wide and is a brilliant, dark purplish-blue with even darker veins. Of the 4 petals, the uppermost lobe is considerably wider than the others. The stems rise 8 to 20 cm high from a slender rootstock. Pairs of leaves, elliptical to egg-like in shape and with nearly smooth margins, are well spaced along the stem. Both the stems and leaves of Alpine Speedwell are covered with fine hairs, and stalks of the flowers are sticky. When the blossom has faded, a heart-shaped seed pod with 2 chambers, not unlike a little locket, remains. Look for this attractive plant in herbmats of the subalpine and alpine zones.

Alpine Forget-Me-Not

BJKWY

Myosotis alpestris [*M. sylvatica*]

BORAGE FAMILY

The fortunate wayfarer who sees the exquisite beauty of this glorious little flower in moist subalpine and alpine meadows does not soon forget the sight. The very fragrant flowers tend to be clumped together when they first bloom, and then lengthen into one-sided racemes with maturity. Each wheel-shaped, azure corolla has a prominent yellow eye. In some areas the corolla may be pink in colour. The 5 stamens are hidden within the corolla tube. This perennial has lance-shaped to linear leaves, the lower leaves having stems but the upper ones attaching directly to the flowering stem. They are covered with long soft hairs, hence the generic name meaning "mouse ear" (from the Greek *mus*, "mouse," and *ous*, "ear"). Alpine Forget-Me-Not is a tiny plant, seldom more than 20 cm tall. It is the official state flower of Alaska.

Low Larkspur

Alpine Speedwell

Alpine Forget-Me-Not

Common Harebell BJKWY

Campanula rotundifolia HAREBELL FAMILY

As implied by the common name, this plant has bell-shaped flowers, several of which are borne on each slender wiry stem. Though the buds are erect, the lovely blue bells usually point outward or hang downward; this protects their nectar and pollen from the rain. Like the clapper of a bell, the style ends in a conspicuous 3-lobed stigma. The stem, 15 to 40 cm tall, has long, narrow, alternate leaves, but the basal leaves, which wither early, are roundish to heart-shaped. The hair-thin stems swing in the lightest breeze and yield to violent gales, but bob up fresh as ever after a storm. An oval-shaped, papery capsule contains the plant's many seeds. Common Harebell is found in a wide variety of habitats from low elevations to the alpine region.

Big Mountain Gentian W

Gentiana calycosa GENTIAN FAMILY

Perhaps the most elegant of all gentians in our area, the huge blue flowers of this plant never fail to arouse admiration. Although they are generally solitary, there may be up to 3 flowers at the tip of a stem 10 to 30 cm high, with 1 or 2 more in each axil of the upper leaves. The long, funnel-shaped corolla is divided into 5 lobes, each separated by a shredded pleat or fold. Each stem is crowded with bright green opposite leaves. These 3-veined leaves are ovate in shape. Big Mountain Gentian grows in clumps at high elevations only in the extreme southern limits of the Canadian Rockies.

Smooth Alpine Gentian BJY

Gentiana glauca GENTIAN FAMILY

Smooth Alpine Gentian is a small perennial of alpine and subalpine meadows. The stems rise 3 to 10 cm from basal rosettes of glossy, yellowish-green leaves. There are also 2 or 3 pairs of leaves along the upright stem. The long, dark blue to greenish-blue blossoms, in a few-flowered terminal cluster, appear unusually large in relation to the size of the plant. The calyx lobes are pointed and unequal in size. This charming little plant prefers to grow in damp, stony places at high altitudes.

Moss Gentian BJW

Gentiana prostrata GENTIAN FAMILY

The most inconspicuous gentian in our mountains, this very small plant, 1 to 10 cm tall, is an annual or biennial with creeping stems. Its tiny, pale green leaves have white margins. The flowers sit alone at the tip of each branch and are usually sky-blue in colour with 4 or 5 pointed petals. These blossoms open only in bright sunshine, closing even when a cloud obscures the sun, or when they are touched. Gentians have been used as medicinal tonics and cleansers since the first century. Alpine tundra and rocky ledges are good places to look for this mite of a plant.

Common Harebell

Big Mountain Gentian

Smooth Alpine Gentian

Moss Gentian

Blue-eyed Grass BJKWY

Sisyrinchium montanum [*S. angustifolium*] IRIS FAMILY

These charming flowers, like gems of azure, are scattered among the grasses of moist meadows from low to moderate elevations. The distinctly flattened stems are 20 to 30 cm in height, about twice as tall as the grass-like basal leaves. Borne in inflorescences carrying up to 5 blooms, each star-shaped flower has 3 virtually identical sepals and petals, each tipped with a minute point, and with a bright yellow eye in the centre. The blossoms wither and droop within a day, to be replaced by fresh ones on the succeeding day. Small black seeds are contained in the globular, 3-parted capsules.

Blue Columbine BK

Aquilegia brevistyla BUTTERCUP FAMILY

Most of our native columbines closely resemble the cultivated varieties found in gardens. Each species is distinctive and easy to identify. Blue Columbine has tall stems, 25 to 50 cm high, skirted at the base by long-stalked, pale green compound leaves, which are divided into several segments. Drooping cream-white and blue flowers hang gracefully at the top of the curving stems. The flower is composed of 5 blue, wing-shaped sepals and 5 creamy white, tube-shaped petals, flaring at the open end with a brush-like tuft of stamens and styles, and tapering to a hooked, bluish spur at the other end. These spurs make a fanciful resemblance to doves perched and facing inward around a drinking dish, the wings being represented by the sepals. Numerous seeds are borne in 5 pods, which are erect at maturity. Blue Columbine is found in meadows, open woods, and rock crevices.

Jones' Columbine W

Aquilegia jonesii BUTTERCUP FAMILY

A dwarf alpine plant, Jones' Columbine stands 5 to 10 cm high on rocky limestone screes. Those who find the plant in full flower will not soon forget its arresting beauty. Each stem produces a single flower which is much larger than other parts of the plant. Both the sepals and petals are generally deep blue or purplish, but white-flowered specimens may be found. In Waterton Lakes National Park some populations have deep-blue sepals ringing cream-coloured petals, resulting in a particularly gorgeous flower. The 5 petals extend backward into a somewhat incurved spur, which may be filled with nectar. Each flower has many stamens and 5 pistils. The lightly hairy, bluish-green leaves, divided into small lobes, are in dense tufts near ground level. This elegant plant is limited in distribution to the extreme southern limits of our area.

Blue Columbine

Blue-eyed Grass

Jones' Columbine

Blue Clematis; Purple Virgin's Bower — BJKWY

Clematis columbiana [*C. occidentalis*] — BUTTERCUP FAMILY

One of only a few climbing or trailing vines found in the Canadian Rockies, Blue Clematis drapes itself over shrubs and herbs and around the trunks of trees. The strong, slender stems produce opposite leaves, each divided into 3 leaflets, between 3 and 7 cm long. Flowers occur singly in the axils of the leaves. These flowers lack true petals, but they attract attention because of the large petal-like sepals, which are showy blue or lavender, accented by darker veining, and sharply pointed. Later in the season the flowers are replaced by a mop of long, greyish-white, fuzzy styles which prolong the beauty of this vine. Open woods and thickets are favoured habitats for this showy plant.

Early Blue Violet — BJKWY

Viola adunca — VIOLET FAMILY

Early Blue Violet is one of the earliest and loveliest of the spring flowers. It is also highly variable in several characteristics. Although most frequently heart- to kidney-like, the leaf shape is variable. Plants may be smooth to densely hairy. A wealth of blue to deep violet flowers, each with a long hooked spur, is set off by the handsome, long-petioled leaves. The 3 lower petals have purple lines and, often, a white base, while the lowermost one is spurred; the 2 lateral petals have white beards. The head of the style is also bearded. These flowers have an exquisite fragrance. This plant is fairly common from dry to shady places at low elevations.

Alpine Harebell — BJ

Campanula lasiocarpa — HAREBELL FAMILY

To find Alpine Harebell in full bloom on a stony slope or scree high above timberline is sufficient reward for even the most arduous hike. Recognizable at once by a single bright bloom of a very rich lilac-blue, the bell-shaped flower, as much as 3 cm long, looks incredibly large compared to the short, slender stem and small leaves. The stem is seldom more than 10 cm tall. The small basal leaves are almost egg-shaped, with a slightly narrow base; the stem leaves are narrower; all are sharply toothed. The seeds are contained in an oval-shaped, papery capsule that is covered with hairs. Seen less often, perhaps because of its short blooming period, is Alpine Bluebell (*C. uniflora*) with smaller, dark blue, trumpet-shaped flowers.

Blue Clematis

Early Blue Violet

Alpine Harebell

Glossary

Achene A dry, one-seeded fruit that does not open when ripe.
Alternate leaves Not opposite; a single leaf at each node.
Annual A plant that completes its lifecycle of germinating, flowering, and ripening seed within one year.
Anther That part of a stamen that bears pollen.
Appressed Lying close or flat against a surface.
Axil The angle between two organs, especially the upper angle between a leaf and the stem.
Basal Located at the base of a plant or of an organ of a plant.
Biennial A plant that completes its life span within two years.
Bract A modified leaf in a flower cluster.
Bulbil A small, usually bulb-like body produced in a leaf axis, that will germinate to produce a new plant.
Calyx The outer floral ring, or sepals, usually green, but sometimes brightly coloured.
Carpel A seed-bearing chamber at the base of the pistil of a flower; the pod of a garden pea is an example.
Corolla The petals or inner floral ring.
Corm A solid bulb; an enlarged base of a stem.
Deciduous Falling off at the end of the growing season; not persistent.
Disk flower The flowers in the central portion of the head in the Composite Family, as distinguished from the ray flowers.
Dissected Deeply and finely cut or lobed into many divisions.
Entire Of a leaf or leaflet, having the margins not at all toothed, lobed, or divided.
Filament The stalk of a stamen below the anther.
Floret An individual small flower, usually one of several in a cluster.
Glabrous Smooth, without hairs.
Glandular Bearing secreting organs or glands.
Herb A plant dying back to the ground at the end of the growing season.
Inflorescence Arrangement of flowers in a cluster.
Involucral Referring to a set of bracts surrounding or just below a flower cluster.
Keel The two lowermost and united petals of members of the Pea Family.
Lanceolate Of a leaf, much longer than wide, broadest near the base and tapering toward the tip.
Legume A name for plants of the Pea Family; also a dry pod-like fruit of the Pea Family, splitting down one or both sides at maturity.
Linear Narrow and nearly uniform in width.
Lobed Cut so as to leave prominent projections.
Node The place on the stem where a leaf is, or was, attached.
Oblanceolate Of a leaf, much longer than wide, broadest part above the middle.
Oblong Longer than broad, having the sides nearly parallel for most of their length.
Obovate Egg-shaped but broadest at top.
Offset A short, prostrate or ascending shoot, usually propagative in function, arising near the base of the plant.

Opposite leaves Situated diametrically opposite each other at the same node.
Ovate Egg-shaped but broadest near the base.
Ovary The part of the pistil of a flower containing the cells that become seeds.
Pappus The tufts of hairs on the achene of many species of the Composite and other families.
Pedicel The stalk of an individual flower.
Perennial A plant which persists for more than two seasons.
Persistent Remaining attached.
Petal One of a whorl of floral organs placed between sepals and stamens, usually brightly coloured.
Petiole The stalk of a leaf.
Pinnate Having two rows of parts or appendages along an axis.
Pistil The female organ of a flower which contains the seeds at maturity.
Pubescence The various types of hairs that cover the surface of a plant.
Raceme An elongated flower cluster, the main stem branching only once, the lowermost flowers opening first.
Ray flower A marginal flower with a strap-shaped corolla in the Composite Family, as distinguished from the disk flowers.
Reduced Smaller in size.
Reflexed Abruptly turned or bent backward.
Rhizome or Rootstock An underground, creeping root-like stem.
Saprophyte A plant which derives its food from non-living organic matter.
Scree Slanting mass of stone fragments at the foot of cliffs or other steep inclines.
Sepal One of the separate parts of a calyx, usually green and leaf-like.
Sessile Without a stalk.
Shrub A woody plant that remains low and usually produces several stems from the base.
Spur A hollow, sac-like extension, usually at the base of certain flowers.
Stamen The pollen-bearing, male organ of a flower consisting of an anther and a filament.
Standard The uppermost petal of a flower in the Pea Family.
Stigma That part of the pistil that receives the pollen.
Stolon A horizontally spreading branch or runner that is inclined to root at the nodes.
Stomata Minute pores in the epidermis of a leaf or stem through which gases and water vapour pass.
Style The attenuated part of a pistil between the ovary and the stigma.
Succulent Fleshy and juicy.
Taproot A prominent vertical root from the main axis of the plant.
Umbel A flower cluster in which all flower stalks arise from one point.
Viscid Sticky, glutinous.
Whorled Set of leaves on the same plane and distributed around the stem.

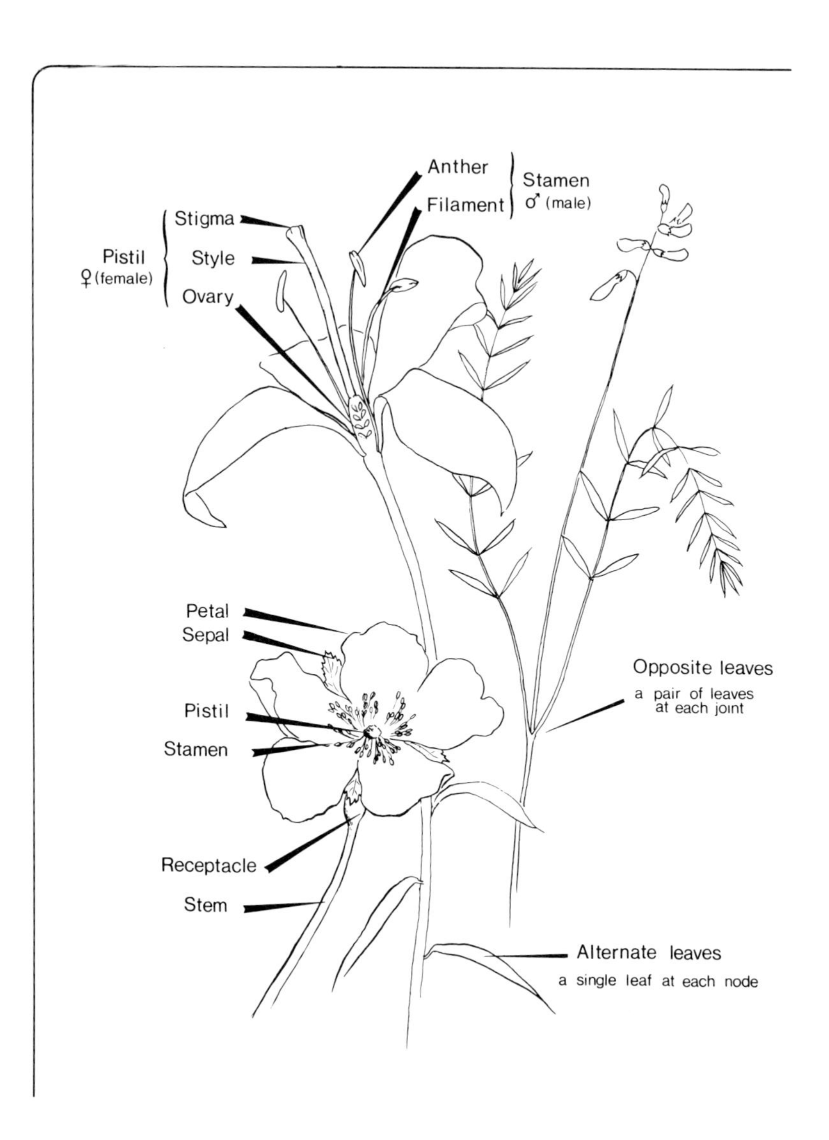

Figure 3. Parts of a typical flower

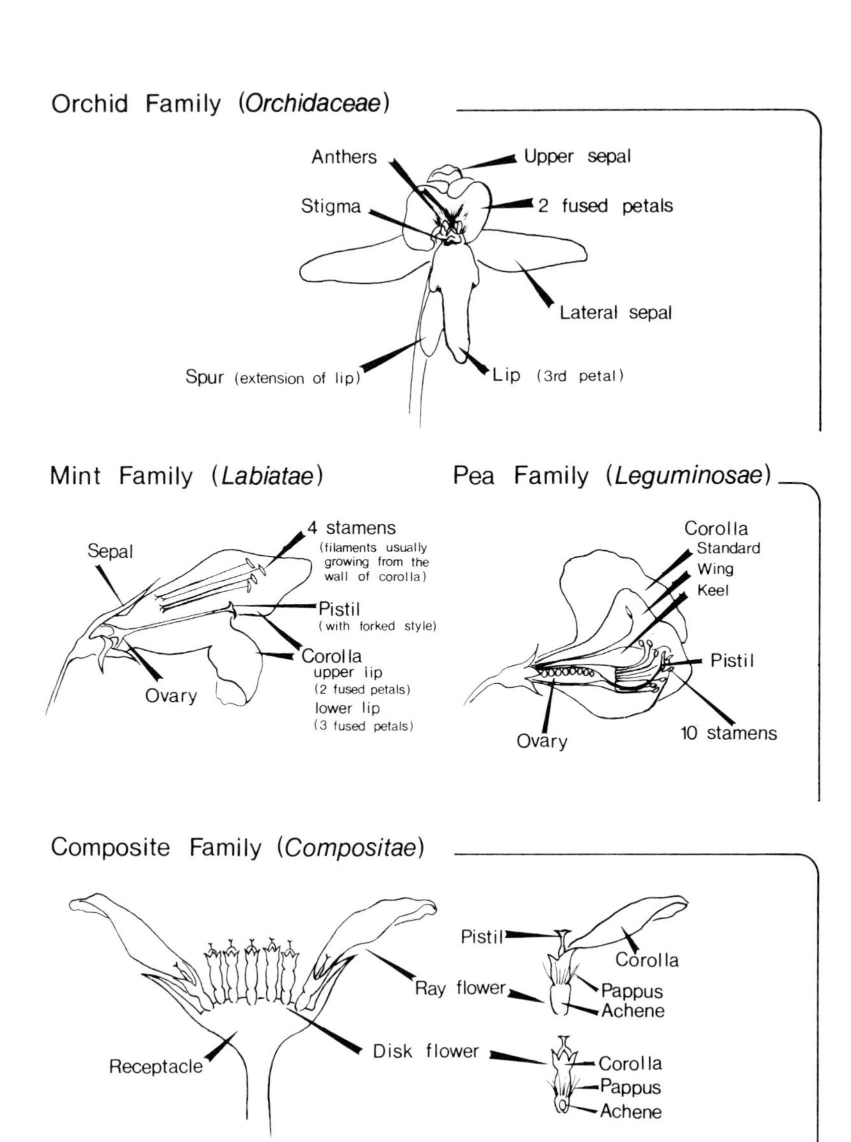

Figure 4. Flower parts in Orchid, Mint, Pea, and Composite families

List of Families

Barberry Family	Berberidaceae
Bladderwort Family	Lentibulariaceae
Borage Family	Boraginaceae
Buckwheat Family	Polygonaceae
Buttercup Family	Ranunculaceae
Composite Family	Compositae (Asteraceae)
Dogbane Family	Apocynaceae
Dogwood Family	Cornaceae
Evening Primrose Family	Onagraceae
Figwort Family	Scrophulariaceae
Gentian Family	Gentianaceae
Geranium Family	Geraniaceae
Grass-of-Parnassus Family	Parnassiaceae
Harebell Family	Campanulaceae
Heath Family	Ericaceae
Honeysuckle Family	Caprifoliaceae
Indian Pipe Family	Monotropaceae
Iris Family	Iridaceae
Lily Family	Liliaceae
Madder Family	Rubiaceae
Mallow Family	Malvaceae
Mint Family	Labiatae (Lamiaceae)
Mustard Family	Cruciferae (Brassicaceae)
Oleaster Family	Elaeagnaceae
Orchid Family	Orchidaceae
Parsnip Family	Umbelliferae (Apiaceae)
Pea Family	Leguminosae (Fabaceae)
Phlox Family	Polemoniaceae
Pink Family	Caryophyllaceae
Poppy Family	Papaveraceae
Primrose Family	Primulaceae
Purslane Family	Portulacaceae
Rose Family	Rosaceae
Sandalwood Family	Santalaceae
Saxifrage Family	Saxifragaceae
Stonecrop Family	Crassulaceae
Sumac Family	Anacardiaceae
Valerian Family	Valerianaceae
Violet Family	Violaceae
Waterleaf Family	Hydrophyllaceae
Wintergreen Family	Pyrolaceae

Selected References

Argus, G. W., and D. J. White. 1978. The rare vascular plants of Alberta—Les plantes vasculaires rares de l'Alberta. *Syllogeus* No. 17. National Museum of Natural Sciences, Ottawa.

Boivin, B. 1967–81. Flora of the prairie provinces. *Memoirs de l'Herbier Louis-Marie.* In 5 parts. Université Laval, Quebec.

Clark, L. J. 1973. *Wild flowers of British Columbia.* Gray's Publishing Limited, Sidney.

Cormack, R. G. H. 1977. *Wild flowers of Alberta.* Hurtig Publishers Ltd., Edmonton.

Craighead, J. J., F. C. Craighead, R. J. Davis. 1963. *A field guide to Rocky Mountain wildflowers.* Houghton-Mifflin Co., Boston.

Harrington, H. D. 1967. *Edible native plants of the Rocky Mountains.* University of New Mexico Press, Albuquerque.

Hitchcock, C. L., and A. Cronquist. 1974. *Flora of the Pacific Northwest.* University of Washington, Seattle.

Hitchcock, C. L., A. Cronquist, M. Ownbey, and J. W. Thompson. 1955–1969. *Vascular plants of the Pacific Northwest.* In 5 parts. University of Washington Press, Seattle.

Hultén, E. 1968. *Flora of Alaska and neighboring territories.* Stanford University Press, Stanford.

Krajina, V. J. 1959. Biogeoclimatic zones and classification of B.C. *Ecology of Western North America,* Department of Botany, University of British Columbia Botany Series No. 1, Vancouver.

Johnston, A. 1970. Blackfoot Indian utilization of the flora of the northwestern Great Plains. *Economic Botany* 24:301–24.

Johnston, A. 1982. *Plants and the Blackfoot.* Natural History Occasional Paper No. 4, Provincial Museum of Alberta, Edmonton.

Johnston, A., S. Smoliak, and R. A. Wroe. 1975. *Poisonous and injurious plants of Alberta.* AGDEX 666-1. Alberta Agriculture, Edmonton.

Kuijt, J. 1982. *A flora of Waterton Lakes National Park.* The University of Alberta Press, Edmonton.

Looman, J., and K. F. Best. 1979. *Budd's flora of the Canadian prairie provinces.* Publication 1662, Research Branch, Agriculture Canada, Ottawa.

Luer, C. A. 1975. *The native orchids of the United States and Canada.* New York Botanical Garden, New York.

Lyons, C. P. 1952. *Trees, shrubs, and flowers to know in British Columbia.* J. M. Dent, Toronto.

Moss, E. H. 1955. The vegetation of Alberta. *Botanical Review* 21:493–567.

Moss, E. H. 1983. *Flora of Alberta.* Second edition revised by J. G. Packer. University of Toronto Press, Toronto.

Packer, J. G., and C. E. Bradley. 1984. *A checklist of the rare vascular plants in Alberta.* Natural History Occasional Paper No. 5, Provincial Museum of Alberta, Edmonton.

Porsild, A. E. 1974. *Rocky Mountain wild flowers.* Natural History Series No. 2. National Museums of Canada, Ottawa.

Scoggan, H. J. 1978. *The flora of Canada*. In 4 parts. Publications in Botany No. 7. National Museum of Sciences, Ottawa.

Simmons, H., and S. Miller. 1982. *Notes on the vascular plants of the Mackenzie Mountain Barrens and surrounding area*. Report No. 3, Northwest Territories Renewable Resources, Yellowknife.

Spellenberg, R. 1979. *The Audubon Society field guide to North American wildflowers, western region*. Alfred A. Knopf Inc., New York.

Stearman, W. A., and G. Wheeler, eds. 1983. *Weeds of Alberta*. AGDEX 640-4. Alberta Agriculture and Alberta Environmental Centre, Edmonton and Vegreville.

Szczawinski, A. F. 1959. *The orchids of British Columbia*. B. C. Provincial Museum Handbook No. 16, Victoria.

Szczawinski, A. F. 1962. *The Heather Family (Ericaceae) of British Columbia*. B. C. Provincial Museum Handbook No. 19, Victoria.

Taylor, T. M. C. 1966. *The Lily Family of British Columbia*. B. C. Provincial Museum Handbook No. 25, Victoria.

Taylor, T. M. C. 1973. *The Rose Family of British Columbia*. B. C. Provincial Museum Handbook No. 30, Victoria.

Taylor, T. M. C. 1974. *The Pea Family of British Columbia*. B. C. Provincial Museum Handbook No. 32, Victoria.

Taylor, T. M. C. 1974. *The Figwort Family of British Columbia*. B. C. Provincial Museum Handbook No. 33, Victoria.

Vance, F. R., J. R. Jowsey, and J. S. McLean. 1984. *Wildflowers across the prairies*. Western Producer Prairie Books, Saskatoon.

Index of Common Names

Index of Scientific Names